MᴄGʀᴀw-Hɪʟʟ's

CAREERS FOR

FOREIGN LANGUAGE AFICIONADOS

& Other Multilingual Types

Careers for You Series

McGraw-Hill's
CAREERS FOR
FOREIGN LANGUAGE AFICIONADOS
& Other Multilingual Types

J. LAURENCE DAY

THIRD EDITION

Mc
Graw
Hill

New York Chicago San Francisco Lisbon London Madrid Mexico City
Milan New Delhi San Juan Seoul Singapore Sydney Toronto

402.373
D
Np2

The **McGraw·Hill** Companies

Library of Congress Cataloging-in-Publication Data

Day, J. Laurence.
      Careers for foreign language aficionados & other multilingual types / by
J. Laurence Day — 3rd ed.
            p.   cm.   — (McGraw-Hill careers for you series)
      ISBN 0-07-148217-2 (alk. paper)
            1. Language and languages—Vocational guidance.   I. Title.

P60.D39   2007
402'.373—dc22   2007010782

1 2 3 4 5 6 7 8 9 10 11 12 13 14 15   DOC/DOC   1 0 9 8 7

ISBN 978-0-07-148217-2
MHID   0-07-148217-2

McGraw-Hill books are available at special quantity discounts to use as premiums and
sales promotions, or for use in corporate training programs. For more information,
please write to the Director of Special Sales, Professional Publishing, McGraw-Hill,
Two Penn Plaza, New York, NY 10121-2298. Or contact your local bookstore.

This book is printed on acid-free paper.

Contents

Foreword

....

D iscover Languages...Discover the World! This phrase captures the essence of the value of this important book, and it is why I was thrilled to be asked to write the Foreword. When a person discovers a new language and learns how to communicate with others from various cultures and communities, that person is discovering an essential life skill that will open up a host of new opportunities. It is through the learning of other languages and cultures that we shrink the size of the world and discover all that it has to offer in terms of travel, cultural exchange, international knowledge, career advancement, and, most importantly, global understanding and tolerance.

In these times, it is becoming increasingly evident that everyone needs to have skills in at least two languages. The countries of the European Union have initiated policies to encourage the teaching and learning of not one but at least two languages in addition to the native language of every citizen of the European Union countries. While people in the European Union and other nations around the world have been learning and continue to learn and speak other languages, Americans lag far behind. Simply recognizing the need to speak other languages is a recent development in the United States and has been focused primarily on issues related to national security. There is, however, small but increasing pressure being brought to bear on local school boards to expand language offerings. More and more parents see the value of an education that includes foreign language instruction beginning at an early age, even prekindergarten, and continuing through high school and college. At the same time, however, school boards have had to cut foreign language offerings in order to pay for the new emphasis on preparation and testing in math and science. The resolution of this tug-of-war is a long way off, and if it is to be resolved in favor of expanding foreign language offerings in our schools, it will require the sustained involvement and advocacy not only of parents, but of business leaders and policy makers at the local, state, and national levels.

And that is the point that brings me back to *Discover Languages...Discover the World!* The American Council on the Teaching of Foreign Languages (ACTFL) has undertaken this long-term public awareness campaign to raise the profile of language teaching and learning in the United States. The ultimate goal of this effort is to increase and sustain the public investment in and support of foreign language education at all levels and for all languages. As stated earlier, certain sectors of the U.S. government recognize the need to expand our language capabilities largely based on national security interests as a result of the terrorist attacks that took place in the United States on September 11, 2001. This is a legitimate and important need, but fighting terrorism focuses mostly on the short term to fix the immediate language deficiencies in our military, homeland security, and international intelligence systems. What we need in addition to this is a long-term and sustained investment in building our nation's educational infrastructure for foreign language teaching in order to ensure our ongoing national security and economic vitality. This infrastructure would involve the development and adoption of policies in agencies such as the Departments of Education, State, Commerce, and Labor that support the teaching of foreign languages in our schools and reward the acquisition of foreign languages by our workforce. Of course, if policies are to be adopted in various government agencies, it will take the active involvement and support of Congress and the White House to move legislation that will enact these policies and the required funding for them.

This brings me to my final point: business. American business, along with our national security interests, can supply the other half of the "one-two punch" we need to get the right policies enacted. While most American businesses—even very small businesses—have become international concerns, there is still very little recognition among business leaders that foreign language and cultural skills are essential for the workforce. Too many American businessmen and women believe that English is the language of business, when, in fact, the language of business is and should be the language of the customer. This is a point that is not lost on business leaders in other parts of the world. The fact is that American business is operating in a language and cultural deficit that has a direct effect on the bottom line.

You, the multilingual type reading this book, are in a great position to help change the attitudes of American business leaders. Should you find a career that uses your language skills, be sure to look for the same skills in others when you, in turn, are in a position to hire. And when you become the executive, encourage your employees to learn other languages and hire people with language skills. And when you meet with other local leaders, school board members, principals, and state and national policy makers, tell them how important it is for your children to have the opportunity to learn other languages to secure the future prosperity of our nation. I wish you good luck and great success!

Bret Lovejoy
Executive Director
American Council on the
Teaching of Foreign Languages
www.discoverlanguages.org

Preface

A s I was preparing to write this preface to the third edition of *Careers for Foreign Language Aficionados & Other Multilingual Types*, I found a newspaper clipping from the *New York Times* that made me wonder if the whole book might soon be superseded by electronic translating devices. The article said that you could buy a talking electronic dictionary and audio phrase book that would translate to or from English, Spanish, French, German, Italian, and Portuguese. I had already logged onto a website that offered to translate—free of charge—blocks of information from dozens of languages to dozens of other languages. Computer chess programs can beat all but the most accomplished world chess masters, so will knowing a foreign language help you get a job or launch a career if any monolingual person can buy a handheld translating gadget? The answer is *si, da, ja, oui, sim*—in other words, yes!

It is true that technology and the leap to cyberspace has changed the way the world functions, but it is important to recognize that while technology helps us navigate in an increasingly complex world, technology isn't our master. Nathan Myrhvold observed in the *New Yorker*, "It is easy to get caught up in technomania and lose sight of the fact that communication, whatever technology carries it, is designed to link human beings." So here's the thing: leading career counselors, corporate headhunters, and job recruiters of all kinds agree that proficiency in a foreign language is a greater asset today than ever before—precisely because technology and cyberspace have made the world a global neighborhood. Because of that, human communication is more important than ever. New jobs are being developed every day for people who speak a second language. If you want to test this statement, log on to an Internet search engine and type "jobs in," then type in the name of a language, any language—Swahili, Urdu, Aymara, Farsi—and you'll find jobs listed. Typing in the name of a common foreign language will bring up search results in the millions.

This book tells you about jobs in volunteer organizations, teaching English as a foreign language, working in major corporations with overseas offices, or working for foreign corporations with offices in the United States. You'll learn that foreign language skills are needed in library and information science, social service, the mass media, entertainment, public relations and promotion, advertising and sales, medical and technical health organizations, travel and tourism, the military, law enforcement and security, and all levels of government. Translating, interpreting, teaching, and consulting are other career options. In this book you will read about people who use their foreign language skills every day in varied and exciting careers. You'll learn how they got their jobs and what they do every day.

If you enjoy words and playing with words, if you like foreign language broadcasts or telecasts, if you enjoy learning about other cultures, you're a step ahead already. Many areas of this global society require foreign language skills. Many career options combine knowledge of a foreign language with some other basic skill or talent. And you don't have to be an office worker to have a satisfying bilingual occupation. Meg Donohue at CareerBuilder.com states that the future is bright for numerous blue-collar positions and that the Bureau of Labor Statistics expects construction and extraction jobs to grow 12 percent by 2014, maintenance and repair jobs by 11.4 percent, and the transportation and material moving industry by increase 11.1 percent. Many of these jobs involve direct contact with people who come from a wide range of cultures and speak a variety of languages. For qualified workers in these job categories, being bilingual would be a definite advantage. With your language skills and your knowledge of two cultures, you can help people communicate with each other. You can help people get the things they want and avoid doing things that would be harmful to them. You can work with foremen, supervisors, and other bosses to help bring about understanding with their foreign language–speaking workers. Knowing a second language and being able to convey information accurately and appropriately in that language will build your self-confidence and self-esteem.

Some people have a gift for languages—they learn the vocabulary quickly and become fluent easily. Other people grow up knowing a second language because it was spoken in their homes. For these fortunate individuals, career opportunities abound, if they approach their goals with a clear plan using accurate, up-to-date information. This book is designed to help provide components for such a plan as well as current career information for those who are already fluent or are well on the way to being fluent in a foreign language. This book will also be valuable for beginning foreign language students who recognize the great career potential that having a second language promises. These people realize that achieving fluency may require considerable effort, but they feel that the rewards are worth it. Whatever your career interests or your level of fluency, you can find ways to use your language skills to advance your objectives.

The book begins with service organizations that accept and need volunteers, often a good place for gaining valuable work experience. The book moves on to service and sales positions then explores opportunities in teaching English as a second language.

It bears repeating that careers in commerce, business, and many blue-collar occupations require specialized training or experience. Knowing a foreign language enhances an applicant's attractiveness to employers. Banking, manufacturing, and consulting firms look for individuals with business savvy and human relations skills. Adding a second language and cross-cultural training to those attributes strengthens a resume considerably.

Information and service careers also demand language skills. Careers in library and information science, health care, human services, mass media and journalism, and the entertainment industry are covered in Chapters 5, 6, 7, 8, and 9.

Chapter 10 shows how people with a yen to see the world, as well as a desire to develop language skills, can find career opportunities in travel and tourism—which will be a growth area as baby boomers retire in the coming decade. Chapter 11 covers jobs at home working for federal, state, and local governments, while Chapter 12 looks at such language-intensive careers as translator, interpreter, or teacher. In Chapter 13, you'll learn the ins and outs of consulting careers. Chapter 1 gives you pointers on enhancing your language skills and experience, and Chapter 14 helps you develop strategies to increase the likelihood of landing jobs that let you use your second language.

CHAPTER ONE

Foreign Language Aficionados

Because the Internet gives you unprecedented access to the current job market, you may feel you don't need this book. However, there's a whole other world out there! The job market has changed dramatically—businesses are now linked instantly by phone, fax, e-mail, and the Web to work sites across some thirty time zones. This book can be a useful tool in that dynamic market. It can also improve your chances of launching a satisfying, fruitful lifetime career.

Until recently, corporations, bureaucracies, and institutions were in charge of your career. Now you are. You define your aspirations and career goals in the way you package your marketable skills. And in today's diverse economic marketplace, people who know foreign languages definitely have a marketable skill.

Some people have a facility for languages, while others struggle valiantly to learn them. The easiest way to learn another language is to live in a home or in a country where that language is being used every day. You hear the same words and phrases so often that eventually they stick. It doesn't take a genius to learn another language; little kids do just fine. Cantinflas, the immortal Mexican comedian, once observed that Americans are very intelligent. "I just returned from a visit to New York," he said, "and even children were speaking English there!"

Fluency in a foreign language is not only possible, it has become much easier to achieve. Tools and opportunities for learning and using a foreign language have never been more abundant. The world keeps getting smaller. It used to take a week bouncing around on the Atlantic Ocean to get from New York to Paris. Nowadays, an airplane will get you there in a few hours. Businesspeople, people visiting relatives, tourists—they all crowd the roads, railways, and airways. Increased travel means greater opportunity and incentive to learn foreign languages.

Those who do master another language find plenty of chances to use their skills. Speaking a second language makes travel easier and more pleasant. And with increased diversity in the United States, people find themselves using foreign language skills closer to home. Anthony Carnevale, one of the nation's leading authorities on education, training and employment, wrote in a recent article that workers at a Washington, D.C., hotel spoke thirty-six languages. Students at a Virginia high school represented seventy-two countries. Opportunities to use foreign language skills on the job are everywhere. And there are career rewards for all types of people who want, or need, to use a language other than their native one.

. . . .

Develop a Plan

Before you go out looking for jobs, it is helpful to determine the level of foreign language skill—and skill in understanding how things are done in other cultures—that you have or are willing to develop. That decision will help you focus on a career choice or employment opportunity that you can realistically achieve. Then you can set short-term goals that put you on track. Aim for a job where your language skills will be an asset. If you speak German, for example, use the Internet to find out about jobs in which knowledge of German will be useful. You'll be amazed at the volume of material available to you with a quick Internet search.

Most job consultants agree that the keys to success for promising employees, regardless of where they work, include a genuine desire to learn and communicate and the self-confidence to make mistakes. Respect for associates' backgrounds also contributes greatly to success. These same qualities also enhance one's ability to learn a foreign language. And fluency in another language, in turn, increases one's communication skills, self-confidence, and appreciation of other languages and cultures. Paul Aron, vice chairperson emeritus of Daiwa Securities America, once said, "English is an international language, but it isn't the international language."

Given all the advantages of knowing a second language, maybe you'll want to add a strategic language to those you already know. For example, Francisco was born in Costa Rica and came to the United States as a young child. He learned Spanish in the home and English outside the home. He studied French in high school and Chinese at the university. Then Francisco volunteered to serve his church for two years in Greece. Francisco's long-term goal was to become a medical doctor and participate overseas with Doctors without Borders.

If you enjoy learning from and communicating with people from diverse backgrounds, a career in which you use a second language may be just right for you. Let's look at some of the possibilities, beginning with those of easiest access and moving on to those that require more training but offer prestige and good salaries.

You may have learned a second language at home or at school, but it is obvious that language facility is aided by some kind of systematic training. However you learned another language, you will want to polish it through study. Nobody can say for sure which language will help you get a job. *All* foreign languages have some market value. You can test this statement by typing "Jobs for Urdu speakers" into an Internet search engine. You'll get the same kind of response for Swahili, Romanian, or Cantonese. In the United States, Spanish has become the dominant language in some cities and a strong factor in communities all over the country. French, German, Portuguese, Italian, Japanese, Chinese, Vietnamese, and Korean are helpful in certain positions. With changes in Eastern Europe and the former Soviet Union, and as economic, social, and political interaction increased, languages from those areas came highly into demand. Modifications of U.S. immigration policies and events in the Middle East and Asia have swelled the opportunity for employees who are fluent in languages from those regions. Francisco, the student mentioned earlier, hopes to be in the vanguard of a multilingual workforce, and two years as a volunteer in Greece helped him with that goal.

Volunteer

Organizations of all kinds these days have connections and activities that spill over borders and across oceans. Civic, fraternal, educational, sports, professional, religious, volunteer groups—all need secretaries and other clerical workers who know at least one language in addition to English. If you have clerical and organizational skills, and the basics of a second language, you can find immediate opportunities to use both.

You may have to volunteer your services to get your foot in the door. However, it will be worth volunteering if you improve your language skills and your understanding of organizations that have international connections. The chance to use your language skills, no matter how limited or undeveloped you may feel they are, is vital. You should recognize that being able to say a few words in your target language, or being able to recognize a few words written in another language, is a skill.

Appendix A gives you information about offices of volunteerism in all fifty states and the provinces of Canada. More information on volunteering is provided in Chapter 2.

Practice

Speaking a language is like playing a musical instrument: practice is the key. Opportunities to get practice in speaking a language abound. Online learning, televised classrooms, and home-study courses have revolutionized the way we learn. Internet guides to distance learning list hundreds of institutions of higher education offering language courses that range, alphabetically, from Aymara to Vietnamese. Hundreds of colleges offer distance learning in Spanish.

The number of foreign language AM and FM radio stations has increased dramatically in the United States. And you may be able to enhance your language skills by watching a movie or soap opera in another language without leaving your house.

Other opportunities to improve your language skills can be found in virtually every town and hamlet in America. Just look at how many different languages are spoken in our own communities. In North American cities, the number of languages spoken other than English often tops one hundred. Between recent immigrants and the many Americans or Canadians who have foreign-born parents and grandparents, the chance that someone nearby speaks your target language is great. It takes some (but not much) effort to find those people, and it takes self-confidence to approach them, but those are the very skills you will want to develop for your career.

You should have a plan. How will you develop the skills you need to succeed in a foreign language career? You may wish to start by getting a realistic picture of the situation you are in now and the resources you have at hand. You already know a little or a lot of some language other than English. How can you improve your chances of using this skill to get a job? How can you improve your language skills? Do you have the funds to take language classes? Can you spend time with people who speak the language?

It doesn't matter what plan you have, as long as you have a plan. It should be logical, taking you from where you are to where you want to be in manageable steps. It should consist of steps that include using the tools you have in order to obtain the skills you need.

Three Keys to Success

Your chances for success will increase if you use three basic concepts as part of your strategy: attitude, opportunity, and effort.

Attitude

The late Paul H. Dunn, speaker and author, told of going to a café in a small town. He asked the waitress what he should order.

She said, "Why don't you try our Enthusiastic Stew?"

"Why do you call it 'Enthusiastic Stew'?" Dunn asked.

"Because we put everything we've got into it," replied the waitress.

Succeeding in a career that uses your second language skills will require your enthusiasm. Enthusiasm is a way of looking at life. Stephen Covey, in his book *Seven Habits of Highly Effective People*, suggests that success comes to people who are proactive. That means they take action, rather than just responding to what happens to them. And they see things that happen to them as opportunities, even when such incidents appear to be negative.

In your career plan, you should include an "attitude checker" that you turn on often to see if your thinking and attitudes are in line with your goals and aspirations. We all get discouraged sometimes, but maintaining a positive, proactive attitude is one key to success.

There is no perfect type of person who can succeed in fields where foreign languages are useful or required. Your personality can be whimsical, plodding, or analytical. What you need to do is build an attitude that will capitalize on your traits and make them work for you.

Opportunity

The Amazon River is one of the largest in the world. When it reaches the sea in eastern Brazil, the fresh water from the Amazon flows far out into the ocean, beyond the sight of land. The story, probably apocryphal, is told of a sailing ship becalmed off the Brazilian coast. Crew members were dying of thirst. They signaled another ship, becalmed in the distance.

"Send us water."

"Let down your buckets where you are," came the signal from the other ship.

"Send us water."

"Let down your buckets where you are."

The thirsty sailors knew it would be fatal to drink seawater, but they did as they were told. They let down the buckets, and to their amazement and joy, the buckets came up filled with fresh water. The ship, though out of sight of land, had sailed into a patch of fresh water that the Amazon River had thrust out into the ocean.

Your career will prosper as you recognize the opportunities to further enhance and develop your second (or third) language skills. These opportunities flourish all around you. You simply have to let down your bucket.

Effort

As you prepare your plan and begin to build your career, be aware that you are the person who will set the level of the career achievement you wish to attain. It's a good idea to look at all goals as worthwhile. There are no good or bad goals as you move forward. There are no high or low goals. There are just goals. There are jobs and career opportunities that require little more effort than showing up for work and having a good attitude. There are career opportunities that require years of training, practice, and the development of specialized skills. The monetary rewards for the latter are usually higher than for the former. But you shouldn't consider only the prestige factors or the monetary rewards. As you make your career plan, think of what will make you happy and then evaluate how much effort it will take to achieve that goal. Plan to make the reward you want match the amount of effort you are willing and able to put into it.

For More Information

There are many resources that can help you develop strategies for getting a job abroad.

Publications

International Job Finder: Where the Jobs are Worldwide (International Job Finder) by Daniel Lauber, 2002.

International Jobs: Where They Are and How to Get Them, 6th ed., by Nina Segal and Eric Kocher, 2003.

Global Resume and CV Guide by Mary Anne Thompson, 2007.

Websites

www.vistawide.com/careers/language_careers.htm

www.go.global.wisc.edu/jobs

Canadian Job Sources

Young Canada Works: Get a job in a field related to your studies in a second official language. These jobs are for college or university students who can speak both English and French. To learn more, visit www.pch.gc.ca/special/ycw-jct/html/welcome_e.htm.

Youth Employment Strategy: This organization helps young people get the skills, knowledge, and work experience needed for a successful career (both official languages). It offers partnership opportunities for employers and includes the Youth Resource Network of Canada, a place to start to find your first job. For more information, visit the website at www.youth.gc.ca/YES.

Council on World Affairs of Canada: This website contains important information and programs for students engaged in the study of world issues through United Nations activities. For information, visit www.cowac.org.

CHAPTER TWO

Volunteer and Service Organizations

I n an article titled "Why Volunteer?" Susan J. Ellis of Energize, Inc., writes that people volunteer for all kinds of reasons but especially to help others. There is a long tradition of volunteering for altruistic reasons, and, according to Ellis, the best volunteering involves a desire to serve others—but that does not exclude other motivations. It is okay, she explains, to want some benefits for yourself from volunteering. In any case, the following anonymous quotation describes the importance of such work: "Volunteers aren't paid—not because their work is worthless, but because it is priceless." Ellis suggests that rather than consider volunteering as something to do for less-fortunate people, you should begin to think of volunteering as a form of exchange. You might volunteer to drive people to their medical appointments for a month, for example, and the next month find yourself being rushed to the hospital emergency room by a volunteer ambulance corps. Volunteering can mean looking out for yourself; for example, you join your neighborhood crime watch, and your home is protected while you protect your neighbors' homes.

Ellis lists about fifty motivations for volunteering, including a number that are pertinent to this chapter: to explore a career, to gain leadership skills, to do your civic duty, to gain recognition, to learn something new, to become an "insider," to be part of a team. Your commitment to volunteering is often strengthened when you can see the benefits to both the recipient of your efforts and to yourself. Consultants say that networking—being in touch with a variety of people—is an important way to move forward socially and professionally. Volunteering is an excellent way to network.

Does your career plan call for you to increase your language and cross-cultural skills before you enter the international job market or before you apply for a job that requires more foreign language skills than you currently have? If so, you may want to volunteer your services to one of the many community organizations or programs that work with people who speak your target language. They may need someone to help with correspondence, answering the telephone, translations, grassroots organizing, writing newsletters, doing research, or fund-raising. Sometimes these positions pay a stipend.

Volunteer Organizations

Volunteer organizations include religious, government, educational, and civic groups. The rest of this chapter is devoted to brief descriptions of a variety of these organizations.

Religious Organizations

Many religious organizations have relief and missionary programs that function overseas. Local congregations, even small towns, often have direct contact with people who live in other countries and speak other languages. Many churches offer programs in their own communities for people who have immigrated to the United States. You might want to participate in networking activities that help these people find assistance for a wide range of problems. You may want to offer to teach classes for these immigrants.

These volunteer tasks provide many opportunities to use your second language and learn about the target culture. Practice oils the tongue; it takes the squeak out of the voice and removes your hesitancy when dealing with people from other cultures.

Most congregations welcome support and cooperation even if you aren't a member of the church. Typically, Christian church groups seek Christian volunteers of any denomination. There are exceptions, however. Jean, a high school student and professed atheist, was welcomed by the local Catholic priest to teach cooking skills to Hmong refugees. All profited from this exchange.

Government Programs

Government agencies are huge employers, and many government programs are involved with service to people. Many of these programs provide excellent employment or volunteer opportunities for people adept with foreign languages.

The Peace Corps. The Peace Corps employs more than 7,700 volunteers, all of whom must be trained in the language of the country to which they are assigned. Since the program began in 1961, more than 187,000 Americans have worked abroad with the Peace Corps in 139 host countries on issues ranging from AIDS education to information technology and environmental preservation. Returning Peace Corps volunteers have found jobs in all kinds of organizations and agencies where knowledge of a foreign language and culture are valued.

Your chances of getting accepted into the Peace Corps are much better if you have a skill that is needed by the participating countries. The Peace Corps looks for a wide range of skills in volunteers: business development, information technology, engineering, medical, and teaching skills are always appreciated. The Peace Corps provides a great opportunity to learn and improve your foreign language skills. For more information, contact:

Peace Corps
1111 Twentieth Street NW
Washington, DC 20526
www.peacecorps.org

AmeriCorps*VISTA. If you would prefer to volunteer in the United States, you may want to consider AmeriCorps*VISTA, which is the domestic counterpart of the Peace Corps. Ameri-Corps is a network of local, state, and national service programs that connects more than seventy thousand Americans each year in intensive service to meet the nation's critical needs in education, public safety, health, and the environment. The organization seeks volunteers who know a variety of foreign languages. You can find more information about the various AmeriCorps programs at www.americorps.org.

USAjobs. USAjobs maintains a website (www.usajobs.com) that allows you to explore more than twenty-three thousand federal jobs. A number of these jobs also require language skills for employees. USAjobs sponsors community action programs in education, legal services, health centers, and programs for migrant workers.

Volunteer Canada. In Canada, more than 161,000 organizations, almost twelve million volunteers, and two million paid staff make up the volunteer and nonprofit sector. Volunteer Canada (*Bénévoles Canada*) offers detailed information about volunteer programs throughout the country. Learn more by contacting:

Volunteer Canada
430 Gilmour Street
Ottawa, ON K2P 0R8
Canada
www.volunteer.ca

Civic Organizations

There are scores of organizations that have as one of their main functions interaction with people and organizations overseas. Many organizations carry out local programs in specific countries and areas of the world. In all likelihood, there is a club, fraternal organization, sister city or people-to-people program, or other group that is involved with local people or people overseas who speak your target language.

North American Civic Groups. Civic organizations throughout North America welcome efforts by members and nonmembers alike who wish to help. Such organizations include Altrusa International, Rotary Club, People-to-People, Amnesty International, Partners of the Americas, Lions Club, Kiwanis, and Sertoma. Some organizations provide stipends or scholarships to study or live abroad. All are interested in promoting international understanding. Other voluntary service organizations are less well known. Some groups focus their efforts on people in North America, many of whom speak little English. Following are several that offer volunteer opportunities.

ACORN volunteers must commit to serving for one year, and they receive a small salary. ACORN prefers English-speaking applicants who also speak Spanish and who have prior experience in grassroots organizing. Work involves organizing low-income communities around issues such as housing, education, and health. For more information, contact:

ACORN
88 Third Avenue
Brooklyn, NY 11217
www.acorn.org

The American Hospital Association has volunteer programs in community service, in-service, fund-raising, and community outreach. You can learn more by contacting:

American Hospital Association
325 Seventh Street NW
Washington, DC 20004
www.aha.org

The General Convention of Sioux Indian YMCAs needs volunteers with camp and/or community development skills to live for four to ten weeks in small, isolated Sioux communities and work on community development projects. For information, contact:

General Convention of Sioux Indian YMCAs
PO Box 218
Dupree, SD 57623
www.siouxymca.org

Habitat for Humanity, the organization that builds homes for low-income people, has a widely diverse organization with a presence in most states. The organization directs a program in Latin America and the Caribbean called Habitat para la Humanidad America Latin y el Caribe. For more information, contact:

Habitat for Humanity International
121 Habitat Street
Americus, GA 31709
www.habitat.org

Los Niños focuses on community development and needs volunteers who can commit to one year. Program areas are school teaching, nutrition, family gardens, and literacy. For information, contact:

Los Niños
287 G Street
Chula Vista, CA 91910
www.losninosinternational.org

The United Farm Workers organization looks for volunteers who can spend one year in rural or urban areas organizing farm workers or consumers. For more information, contact:

United Farm Workers
PO Box 62
Keene, CA 93531
www.ufw.org

Universal Giving is a social entrepreneurship nonprofit dedicated to making giving and volunteering a natural part of everyday life. The Web-based service connects donors and volunteers with organizations all over the world. The service promotes both giving and volunteering. For information, contact:

Universal Giving
560 Sutter Street, Suite 210
San Francisco, CA 94102
www.universalgiving.org

VolunteerMatch is dedicated to helping everyone find a place to volunteer. The organization offers a variety of online services to support nonprofit, volunteer, and business leaders committed to civic engagement. It serves more than forty thousand charitable organizations. To learn more, contact:

VolunteerMatch
717 California Street, Second Floor
San Francisco, CA 94108
www.volunteermatch.org

Volunteering Abroad. Some organizations focus on other countries, especially developing countries. Examples of these groups follow.

The American Friends Service Committee cosponsors six- to eight-week summer projects involving construction, gardening, arts and crafts, and child care. Fluency in Spanish is usually required. For more information, contact:

American Friends Service Committee
1501 Cherry Street
Philadelphia, PA 19102
www.afsc.org

Founded in 1965 in Houston, Texas, Amigos de las Americas seeks volunteers with at least one year of high school Spanish to work in health clinics in Latin America. For information, contact:

Amigos de las Americas
5618 Star Lane
Houston, TX 77057
www.amigoslink.org

Brethren Volunteer Service, affiliated with the Church of the Brethren, sponsors a wide range of community development projects in Latin America, the Caribbean, the Middle East, Europe, and China. Most tours are for one to two years. For more information, contact:

Brethren Volunteer Service
451 Dundee Avenue
Elgin, IL 60120
www.brethrenvolunteerservice.org

Hunger-relief and health programs in Bangladesh, Mexico, Central America, Sierra Leone, and the Sudan are the focus of Concern America. The group seeks volunteers with a degree in public health, nutrition, agriculture, engineering, or medicine. Placements are for a minimum of one year. For information, contact:

Concern America
PO Box 1790
Santa Ana, CA 92702
www.concernamerica.org

Friends of the Orphans supports three thousand children in Bolivia, the Dominican Republic, El Salvador, Guatemala, Haiti, Honduras, Mexico, Nicaragua, and Peru through a network of orphanages. Through fund-raising and volunteer efforts, they support the orphanages of Nuestros Pequeños Hermanos (NPH), Spanish for Our Little Brothers and Sisters. They need volunteers in construction and food preparation and as dorm directors. Placements are for one year. Room and board are provided. For more information, contact:

Friends of the Orphans
85 West Algonquin Road, Suite 395
Arlington Heights, IL 60005
www.friendsoftheorphans.org

SCI International Voluntary Service sponsors projects in rural development (agriculture, public health, small enterprise, cooperative development, organizational management) throughout the world. Volunteers choose from participation in short-term (two to three weeks) international work camps or long-term (three months or more) volunteer opportunities in more than sixty countries. For more information, contact:

SCI International Voluntary Service
5505 Walnut Level Road
Crozet, VA 22932
www.sci-ivs.org

Operation Crossroads Africa operates self-help projects in community development in more than forty African countries.

Knowledge of French is required for some of the assignments. The program fee in 2007 was $3,500 and covered airfare, in-country transportation, visas, health insurance, food, and housing costs for the seven-week summer program. For information, contact:

Operation Crossroads Africa
PO Box 5570
New York, NY 10027
www.operationcrossroadsafrica.org

World Teach is a nonprofit, nongovernmental organization that provides opportunities to live and work as volunteer teachers in developing countries. It sends college graduates to Africa, Costa Rica, China, Thailand, Poland, and other countries to teach for one year (usually English) in secondary school. It costs volunteers between $1,000 and $5,000, depending on the country, to cover the costs of training and housing, but some countries provide a monthly stipend.

World Teach
c/o Center for International Development
Harvard University
79 JFK Street
Cambridge MA 02138
www.worldteach.org

Most of these organizations operate with extremely low over-head. When requesting information of these agencies, it is a good idea to enclose a few dollars to help cover mailing expenses.

A Word of Advice About Volunteering

You are following your plan to develop your language skills and launch yourself into an interesting, fruitful career. It is good to remember your overall goal at all times. It is also important to set short-term goals and to undertake activities that will help make your long-term goals successful. To do that, you must really be interested in the people and projects of the organization where you work.

Remember to put the organization's purpose high on your list of priorities. If you approach volunteerism with a selfish attitude and think, "I'll do this because I can see how it will help me, but I won't do that because that won't help me," you will probably not be successful. Think it through. Learn to accept assignments enthusiastically. Look for what is needed and begin to do those things that will help your group or organization succeed.

For example, Rebecca had always been interested in Ethiopia. She hadn't had the chance to learn Amharic or any of the other languages spoken there, but she was willing to try. She noticed that there were lots of Ethiopian restaurants in a nearby city. After asking some questions of the people who ran several of the restaurants, Rebecca volunteered to be an aide in a preschool program that catered to Ethiopian children while their parents worked. After a year she had become functional in Amharic just from hearing it all day long from the children and their teachers. She was then invited to continue—as a paid aide.

Volunteering is an excellent way to improve your fluency and job experience, but you should choose an organization whose mission is truly important to you.

For More Information

Excellent sources of more detailed information on these and other agencies may be found in your local library; some are listed below.

Career Opportunities in the Nonprofit Sector by Jennifer Bobrow Burns, 2006.

Connections: A Directory of Lay Volunteer Service Opportunities
St. Vincent Pallotti Center
Cardinal Station, Box 893
Washington, DC 20064
www.pallotticenter.org

Directory of International Internships: A World of Opportunities
Michigan State University
Career Services and Placement
113 Student Services Building
East Lansing, MI 48824
www.isp.msu.edu/students/internships/intlguide

International Workcamps & Voluntary Service Projects Directory
Volunteers for Peace
1043 Tiffany Road
Belmont, VT 05730
www.vfp.org

Council on International Education Exchange (CIEE)
7 Custom House Street, Third Floor
Portland, ME 04101
www.ciee.org

CHAPTER THREE

Teaching English as a Second Language

E llen Lewin never thought she'd be a teacher of English as a second language (ESL), the former VISTA volunteer wrote in an article on the TESOL website. But she followed her husband to Mexico, where he had a job in a new English school. The school hired Ellen because she was a native English speaker. Ellen struggled a lot. She realized that being a native English speaker hadn't prepared her to *teach* English, so she started formal study of ESL and liked it. "Since then, I have tried other jobs in the 'real world,' but nothing is as fun as ESL!" wrote Ellen.

Nearly thirty million foreign-born people reside in the United States, according to statistics published by the National Institute for Literacy. That's more than 10 percent of the total U.S. population. Among the foreign born in 2000, 51 percent were born in Latin America, and 25.5 percent were born in Asia. A combined total of more than 75 percent of foreign-born U.S. residents speak Latin American or Asian languages. Canada's population in 2007 was thirty-three million. Of that population, 18.4 percent—about six million—were foreign born, according to Statistics Canada. In communities all over North America, new immigrants arrive to work and raise their families, just as they have throughout recent history. This continuing stream of immigration stimulates the economy and creates many opportunities for those who can teach English to speakers of other languages.

If you think you would enjoy teaching English as a second language, several options are open to you. Public and private schools at all levels need teachers. Businesses and community groups seek English as a second language (ESL) and English as a foreign language (EFL) teachers to help adults gain fluency in English. There are English language institutes, American schools abroad, and opportunities to tutor students privately. Whether you want to work with preschoolers or senior citizens, in the United States or abroad, there are always opportunities to teach English.

Preschool, Primary, and Secondary Schools

Our public and private schools often provide classes in English as a second language to students who have not yet developed sufficient fluency in English. This is a school's most common response to students who are just learning English. Many schools go even further. They offer bilingual education, teaching subject matter in the student's native language (so the student won't fall behind in science, math, and social studies) while also teaching English as a second language. Reading and writing skills are often taught in both languages.

Community Colleges and Universities

Most colleges like to have international students matriculate for two reasons. First, they enrich the campus social and cultural life, providing American students with broadening experiences of other cultures and peoples. Second, they are a substantial source of income for the colleges. Non-English-speaking students generally have to pass an English language proficiency test (TOEFL— Test of English as a Foreign Language) before they are admitted to a degree program. Since many students arrive without the required level of English fluency, many colleges offer intensive programs in English for these students so they can do well academically and participate fully in the life of the college. ESL courses offered to international students are frequently multicultural, with individuals from different ethnic and national origins enrolled.

Survival English

Adults in the community who are learning English as a second (or third) language have immediate needs that must be met quickly. Learning enough English to survive in the United States is one of the most important of those needs. Survival requires being able to communicate in emergencies to police, firefighters, health workers, and school administrators. It means filling out a job application and being able to read safety signs at the workplace. Survival requires skill in buying food at the supermarket, using public transportation, or getting a driver's license. For some immigrants, basic literacy is an immediate need.

These are the kinds of issues that ESL teachers focus on while teaching adults. These ESL classes are generally offered in the evenings. They provide a part-time source of income to ESL teachers, most of whom find the work exceptionally rewarding. It is fun to teach English to motivated adults from other lands. One Los Angeles ESL teacher put it this way: "These are special people, and they capture your heart."

English for the Workplace

The education level of many immigrants is several years higher than for North Americans in general. Still, many immigrants arrive with only a few years of primary education. Those without marketable technical skills, as well as well-educated immigrants lacking English skills, often find work in food service at restaurants or hotels. They may find jobs as taxi drivers or housekeepers. Wherever the work, learning English is usually an advantage.

Sometimes a corporation will offer ESL classes to its employees. These classes develop skills in using the kind of English that the workers need. Construction workers learn a different set of vocabulary from cab drivers. These ESL courses benefit both businesses and employees, and they may provide the perfect teaching opportunity for you.

English has become the international language of many professions: airline pilots and air controllers, businesspeople, and diplomats. In many fields of study, especially technical areas, the only available textbooks are written in English. The result is that there are many people in the United States, Canada, and other countries of the world who would like to learn some English in order to pursue their professions. This provides work opportunities for you if you would like to teach ESL, either in North America or abroad.

American Schools Abroad

Most private schools abroad teach students English. Even American schools enroll students who are just learning English. The American School in Guatemala, for example, enrolls about 15 percent Americans; the rest are mostly Guatemalans. Of the 85 percent who are nonnative speakers of English, many are struggling with English. American schools abroad need dynamic people with experience teaching ESL. The schools generally require a teaching certificate from some state in the United States.

Investigating these teaching opportunities may be easier than you would think. Six years ago, entering "Teaching English Abroad" into a major Internet search engine produced 133,000 listings. In 2007, the same phrase yielded 1.2 million listings.

English Language Institutes

Every urban area of the world has privately run language schools, and English inevitably is one of the languages offered. Frequently, North American tourists looking to prolong their stay in an interesting port of call will drop by these establishments and inquire into the possibility of employment. Usually the openings are for part-time teachers and the pay is modest—barely enough to live on, if your needs are simple. But this is a wonderful way for you to meet people and get better acquainted with the country and to help pay for the experience.

The U.S. Department of State's English Language Programs and U.S. embassies work with three types of English language programs outside the United States: Binational Centers, U.S. Embassy English Teaching Programs, and U.S. Embassy Affiliated English Teaching Programs. The Bureau of Educational and Cultural Affairs website, which is part of the U.S. Department of State, states that the Office of English Language Programs does recruit and hire English language teachers for its programs, but it invites people interested in teaching in its programs to send inquiries directly to the specific program in the country where you wish to teach. These programs usually hire teachers who are already in the country, pay local wages and benefits, and typically do not provide international travel or benefits.

Bruce had always wanted to spend a few years in Greece, and prior to visiting, he wrote to the director of the binational center there, enclosing a resume and indicating that he would be in the country for a visit on a set date and would call to arrange a meeting. Bruce not only got a job as an ESL teacher, but things worked out so well that he became the center's director of curriculum several years later.

Finding opportunities in Greece (or Indonesia, for that matter) will be easier for you than it was for Bruce. All you have to do is type "Office of English Language Programs" into any major Internet search engine. You can access lists of overseas centers and a lot of other useful information.

Private Tutoring

People who can afford it often hire a tutor to teach them or their family members English. They find tutoring is a convenient way to learn the language. The tutor goes to the student's home and teaches for an hour or two at a time, once or more a week. In some countries, this can provide a reasonable living for an ESL teacher. One ESL teacher in Tokyo taught English to various members of the same family for twenty years. More recently, another ESL teacher, Seth, taught English in Tokyo for three years while he prepared for graduate school in business in a U.S. university.

Qualifications

Wherever you work, employers look for two major qualifications in ESL/EFL teachers. The first requirement is training in the techniques of teaching English to speakers of other languages. The other qualification is actual experience in teaching English as a second language. Both are important to your success as an ESL/EFL teacher.

Naturally, the more training you have, the more marketable you become. Some jobs, like those in colleges, generally require a graduate degree in ESL, sometimes a Ph.D. Most intensive English programs would like you to have experience abroad. Some insist on it. Jobs in public primary and secondary schools usually require state teacher certification. It is still possible, however, for someone with just a bachelor's degree to land a job as an ESL teacher. And jobs as teachers' aides generally do not require more than a high school education.

Often prospective employers seek those with two or three years of experience teaching ESL. This creates the classic dilemma: How do you get experience if employers want people who already have experience? As the late Ray Charles put it in one of his songs, "How you get the first is still a mystery to me." Still, you can meet the catch-22 requirement for prior experience in several ways. Consider starting as a volunteer in a private agency's program (see Chapter 2), work as a teacher's aide, or plan to graduate from a program that includes a teaching practicum.

John, an English major who enjoyed working with people from other cultures, wanted to learn Russian, but his college didn't offer it. During summer break, at the end of his junior year, John made arrangements to work for room and board as an ESL teacher's aide in a summer program in the former Soviet Union, gaining the chance to learn the language and experience the culture.

In addition to teaching experience and knowledge of ESL methods, two other major qualifications are often sought: knowledge of a foreign language and experience living in another culture. ESL teachers can anticipate the specific problems their students may experience if they know the students' native language. For instance, if the student speaks Spanish, the teacher knows that the American *r* sound, the *th,* and the short *i* sounds will give the student some trouble. Sometimes it is not practical to speak the student's language because there may be twenty different languages represented in one classroom. Even so, having experienced the process of learning a foreign language themselves helps teachers understand the students' problems.

Experience living in another culture is also helpful for ESL teachers. It improves a teacher's accent and increases fluency to use the language on a daily basis with native speakers. And knowledge of another culture can help ESL teachers better educate and understand their own students. In addition, assignments abroad are easier to land if the employer knows that the teacher is comfortable living in other countries and enjoys experiencing a new culture.

Opportunities and Rewards

Opportunities to experience a new culture while teaching English as a foreign language abroad or to work as an adult literacy or remedial education teacher are expected to grow. Employment is expected to increase as fast as the average for all occupations through 2014, and a large number of job openings is expected as institutions replace people who leave for other jobs or retire.

Employers now require a more literate workforce. Demand for adult literacy, basic education, and secondary education classes continues to grow. Significant employment growth is anticipated, especially for ESL teachers. Earnings are increasing, too. Median hourly earnings of adult literacy and remedial education teachers were around $20 a hour in 2007. The lowest-paid teachers were earning more than $10 an hour, and the highest-paid teachers received $30 to $35 an hour.

For More Information

Sources of information on careers in teaching English as a second language are listed below.

ESL in Canada
20 Bloor Street East
PO Box 75117
Toronto, ON M4W 3T3
Canada
www.eslincanada.com

U.S. State Department
Bureau of Educational and Cultural Affairs
2201 C Street NW
Washington, DC 20520
www.state.gov

National Association for Foreign Student Affairs (NAFSA)
Association of International Educators
1307 New York Avenue NW, Eighth Floor
Washington, DC 20005
www.nafsa.org

Center for Applied Linguistics
4646 Fortieth Street NW
Washington, DC 20016
www.cal.org

Institute of International Education
809 United Nations Plaza
New York, NY 10017
www.iie.org

TESOL (Teachers of English to Speakers of Other Languages)
700 South Washington Street, Suite 200
Alexandria, VA 22314
www.tesol.edu

Most states and many foreign countries have TESOL affiliates.

CHAPTER FOUR

Commerce and Business

Every business model has been turned upside down and inside out by the Internet and e-commerce. It's a very volatile marketplace, but thousands of Internet businesses are created every year, and many of them survive and thrive. By staying innovative and forward thinking, entrepreneurs have created new companies and provided new jobs for thousands of people. In these revolutionary times, it pays to think outside the box. To be successful and advance in your career, you must make yourself valuable to the company, especially if the company is your own.

All Business Is Global

Now more than ever, making yourself valuable may involve developing your language and cross-cultural capabilities to go along with a marketable skill because commerce has gone global. Business is conducted in hundreds of languages twenty-four hours a day in some thirty time zones. Workers who are cross-culturally aware and linguistically adept are needed. Global businesses need workers with creativity and enterprise as much as those with technical skills. Because of the Internet, the term *global* applies to business endeavors that a decade ago were strictly local. *Think locally, act globally* applies to small hotels in the Ozarks as well as to multinational conglomerates.

Members of this new global workforce create, analyze, and disseminate goods and services from Punta Arenas to Helsinki and from Gabarone to Shanghai in languages that range from Aymara to Zulu. The information technology (IT) workforce is complex and growing, according to the Computing Research Association. Job growth in information technology has exploded, and higher education has expanded instruction degree offerings. The scores of programs that focus on training people for jobs in information technology range from the sciences to the humanities. There are many different jobs involving widely varying skill and knowledge sets. These jobs are distributed across many sectors of the economy. One constant in this complexity is that foreign language proficiency is among the valued knowledge sets. Maria Schafer, a human capital management specialist, writes, "A white-hot global economy driven by a high-powered technology engine is propelling IT jobs to the center of attention at organizations worldwide."

What does that mean to you, a foreign language aficionado with cross-cultural capabilities? It means that in your job, whatever it may be, you may be working side by side with someone from another culture whose first language is not English.

As companies jockey for position in the global marketplace, they seek clear, consistent, and continual communication between and among employees and management. With your language and cross-cultural skills, you can be a valuable asset in your company's nonstop effort to build awareness and understanding of the company's culture.

Government regulations now require business and commerce to provide workers with time off for a variety of family-related matters. As a result, the number of temporary or part-time jobs as well as full-time at-home jobs that use an array of telecommunication systems has grown rapidly. Thus, in an ever-more ethnically and culturally diverse society, where temporary and sales jobs are flourishing, your linguistic and cross-cultural skills could help you gain employment and promotions.

Modern businesspeople realize the economic necessity of doing business abroad. Overseas assignments are becoming increasingly important to advancement within executive ranks. The executive stationed in another country no longer need fear being out of sight and out of mind. He or she can be sure that the overseas effort is central to the company's plan for success and that promotions often follow or accompany an assignment abroad. If an employee can succeed in a difficult assignment overseas, superiors will have greater confidence in his or her ability to cope back in the United States or Canada, where cross-cultural considerations and foreign language issues are becoming more and more prevalent. Small businesses in the United States are getting into markets where the medium of exchange is the mark, the yuan, the yen, the peso, or the pound.

Paul has a home in a small Midwest city and works out of the office of a small janitorial firm in Salt Lake City. He spends part of his time in Shanghai and Beijing overseeing the sales in the company's subsidiary business—cement polishing.

Large corporations have international branches or divisions, and they deal with foreign investors and buyers on a daily basis. Topeka, Kansas, is the world headquarters of a shoe retailing firm whose shoes are manufactured in China and sold throughout the United States, Latin America, and the Caribbean.

Bill is a chemist who works for a paint manufacturing company. His university minor was French. Bill's company sent him to Africa for three years, partly because of his language capability, then promoted him when he returned.

The employee posted abroad who speaks the country's principal language has an opportunity to fast-forward certain negotiations and can have the cultural insight to know when it is better to move more slowly. The employee at the home office who can communicate well with foreign clients is an obvious asset. Such people build a niche for themselves in the firm. They find they are included in the loop in which key company business is discussed and decided.

. . . .

Languages

According to foreign language consultants, the leading languages that will be vital to U.S. and Canadian business success in the next two decades are Spanish, Chinese, French, Arabic, Japanese, Russian, and German. However, even more languages can be included in the list. There are about twenty industrialized nations, and knowledge of the native languages of these countries can be a real advantage to a businessperson.

The business practice of outsourcing certain company functions has increased the number of individuals who may be based locally but have daily interaction with company representatives overseas. Industrialized nations do not trade exclusively with other industrialized nations. Rising incomes and expectations bring markets for North American goods and services to nonindustrialized countries around the world, and it is easier to sell something to someone if you speak his or her language.

Asian languages are vital to the new economic mix. The United States imports billions of dollars worth of merchandise annually from China, Taiwan, Korea, and Japan. And the entrepreneur with Russian or German or Chinese language skills—or the corporation with employees fluent in those languages—has an advantage. With so many choices, which languages should you study to advance your business career? Of course, the answer depends on your individual interests and aspirations. However, Spanish rates as the second language of the world and is, after English, the language most spoken in forty-seven of the fifty states. If you are looking for a career language that has high potential, Spanish may be it. Spanish can be easier to learn than some other languages because Spanish classes are offered in virtually every U.S. town, and you can easily find native speakers of Spanish to converse with. Demographic projections show that the percentage of native Spanish-language speakers will increase dramatically in the next two decades in the United States. With that rise in Spanish speakers will come an increase in the need for people who speak both English and Spanish and are comfortable with cultural realities of both societies.

Teaching Languages to Businesspeople

Many business schools have begun to integrate foreign language requirements into their programs as they recognize the importance of language skills to their graduates' success in the outside world. Some companies take the position that it is easier to teach a good businessperson a second language than it is to teach a language-skilled individual how to succeed in business.

That fact in itself offers career opportunities. Jobs and business opportunities are available for people who know other languages and can teach them effectively to business school students and business executives who travel abroad.

Setting aside for the moment the language programs of universities and colleges, there are many organizations that teach intensive language courses on a commercial basis. Some of these courses consist of ten one-hour sessions. The students learn grammar, usage, and cultural skills. Such organizations offer jobs and career opportunities for teachers, office personnel, and curriculum specialists who recognize the importance of cross-cultural understanding and nonverbal nuances in communicating with students.

Culture camps and workshops are another offshoot of the growing need for knowledge of foreign languages in commerce and industry. Language "cramming" is only part of the curriculum of culture camps; another important element is etiquette in the target society. This training makes it easier to move into target cultures without making a serious faux pas. Jobs at culture camps would be similar to those in language schools, but the camps put special emphasis on foreign cultural practices.

Job List

Following is a list of jobs in banking, manufacturing, and consulting firms and in multinational corporations. Some of these positions require knowledge of a foreign language, but most do not. Even though the words *second language required* currently appear on relatively few business and industrial job descriptions, the realities of the business world strongly imply a need for language skills. It is up to you to recognize these implications and build your language skills in order to land a position or prepare for a career.

You should also note that this list is by no means inclusive. For every industry, and for virtually every company, there are infinite variations of requirements and expectations. Even in jobs requiring the most basic skills, the ability to communicate well can be the key to advancement.

Computer and Information Systems

Almost everything we deal with these days is computerized—cars, television sets, microwave ovens, wristwatches, cash registers. The list is almost endless. The United States exports computers, computer software, and computer components. Thus, language skills are often used in these positions:

Computer engineer
Independent consultant
Information archivist
Information technology (IT) security specialist
Interactive media specialist
Intranet developer
IT management recruiter

Network architect
Online gaming sales manager
Technical support specialist
Telecommunications technician
Web business development specialist
Web content developer

Banking and Financial Services

Banking is the grandfather of international commerce. Banking executives and bank employees play well-established and long-standing roles in the field. What is new is the amount of bilingual and multicultural business coming into routine banking activities and procedures. In the following positions, language skills can prove valuable:

Certified Financial Planner (CFP)
Teller
Loan officer
Private banking specialist
Financial services sales specialist

Advertising and Public Relations

The U.S. and Canadian advertising business grew enormously during the economic expansion following the turn of the twenty-first century. The introduction of e-commerce advertising added depth and new dimensions to the industry at home and overseas. Opportunities in advertising will be more fully discussed in Chapter 7, but for the purposes of this chapter, advertising positions break down into the following major areas:

Advertising account executive
Advertising copywriter
Digital producer
Direct response marketing specialist

Environmental public relations specialist
Flash developer
Graphic project coordinator
New media designer
Public relations manager
Special events marketer
Web designer

Human Resources and Employee Services

Whether in North America or in the foreign division of a multi-national corporation, human resources departments play a role of importance. Coordinating the needs and expectations of the company and employees helps move the company forward.

Following are positions that are increasingly being filled by language-qualified people:

Benefits specialist
Career counselor
Employee assistance program counselor
Human resources manager
International human relations consultant
Research coordinator

Customer Care

All businesses depend on customer service employees who can handle requests of all kinds and take care of a variety of problems. Companies often depend on off-site specialists working with computers and telephone networks to provide this service with speed, accuracy, and diplomacy. Foreign language skills are always an asset in these jobs.

Following are positions in customer service:

Manufacturer's representative
Online customer-care representative
Product service consultant

Product support specialist
Receptionist
Web sales representative

Product Management and Marketing Research

In these days of e-commerce and global markets, it would be difficult to think of any job that is closer to the heart of a company than that of product management and marketing. In business, media, and entertainment fields, emerging technologies are rapidly transforming the landscape. Multimedia technologies, virtual reality, high-definition television, and flat-panel displays have transformed images, sound, and text into nonlinear, interactive communication. The commercial media have moved away from passive content delivery toward targeted message transmissions that solicit consumer responses. Thus, product managers and marketers have to understand the receptiveness of consumers. For this reason, there is an increasing interest in workers who have foreign language skills and who are cross-culturally adept. For careers in this field, computer and statistical capabilities are essential, and research skills are vital. According to experts, problem formulation, data collection, data analysis and interpretation, and communication abilities are skills people use every day in product management and marketing.

Here are some career areas and job categories in this growing field:

Brand manager
Database marking manager
Design engineer
International sales trainer
Marketing staff editor
Marketing staff writer
Product manager
Product engineer

Promotions coordinator
Sales and marketing representative
Supply chain system specialist
System specialist

These lists just break the surface of jobs available in business for people with language skills. Banking, retail, manufacturing, and advertising have all gone multinational, and many require second languages of their employees.

For every position mentioned, dozens more exist or are being created. And while knowledge of a second language may not be a prerequisite to employment, knowing a foreign language can help you stand out in a group of monolingual job applicants. The best advice in the business area is to gain a specific skill and take steps to learn a language that will enhance your value to a company.

The best strategy usually calls for getting a job with a firm that does business abroad, then positioning yourself within the company for an overseas assignment. That way you get paid in dollars at what is usually a higher salary rate than that paid for comparable jobs in the host country.

Opportunities and Rewards

The *Occupational Outlook Handbook* predicts that employment of computer support specialists will increase faster than the average for all occupations through 2014 as organizations continue to adopt increasingly sophisticated technology and integrate it into their systems. Job growth will continue to be driven by ongoing expansion of the computer system design and related services industry. Software publishing jobs have more than doubled since the 1990s, and earnings in this area have been markedly higher than in industry and commerce as a whole. Software publishing is projected to be the third fastest growing industry in the U.S. economy over the next decade.

General and operations managers earned around $37 an hour in 2007. Per-hour pay in the software publishing industry was $20 an hour higher than in industry and commerce in general. Computer and information system managers in commerce and industry were making about $45 an hour. Earnings ranged down from there in the various job categories to customer service representatives, who earned around $15 an hour.

For More Information

Here are some job search resources available on the Internet:

www.accentjobs.com
Based in New York City; places financial professionals and provides administrative and temporary support personnel to national and international firms

www.latpro.com
Online job board launched in 1997 for Hispanic and bilingual professionals

www.multilingualvacancies.com
European bilingual recruitment network; seeks to connect progressive companies with qualified career-minded individuals

CHAPTER FIVE

Library and Information Science

On a recent November night in Colorado, the Boulder Public Library's Multi-Cultural Outreach Services presented "There Was and There Was Not: Wonder Tales of the Islamic World" in its Children's Theater Series. In another part of the library, the Arabic Literature Discussion Group was meeting. Among the library's ongoing programs are citizenship classes and weekly Spanish conversation classes.

Public libraries are often in the forefront of multilingual, cross-cultural activities in cities and towns across America. In addition, public libraries provide a vast array of information in a personal and private work space. In this information age, more new information is produced around the world each day than used to be produced in centuries. It is impossible to keep track of all of this information, but libraries and librarians help the world cope with it.

Information is power. Those with the technical and artistic skills to sift through the glut of data and extract the relevant tidbits required by a client or employer are increasingly valuable to society and, more to the point of this book, valuable to their employers. This is the expertise of the librarian and the information researcher.

Libraries exist in all parts and levels of our society and go by many names: media centers, electronic databases, archives, and information centers. A library by any other name is still a library: a storehouse of information.

As the global store of information continues to expand, there will be a greater and greater need for specialists—librarians who can create, manage, administer, and utilize both their own information and the information of related businesses and institutions. As the world shifts to electronic rather than print resources, some have predicted a decline in the need for libraries and librarians because so much of the world's information is becoming available online. Not so. The larger and more complex the system, the greater the need for skilled and trained professionals to make sense of the information, and one of the key factors in the growing globalization of information systems is language. Libraries will continue to be gateways to the world's information storehouse, and multilingual librarians will be necessary and valuable guides for their patrons, colleagues, and employers.

Types of Libraries

The usefulness of multiple language skills will depend on your job title and the type of library where you work. There are basically four types: public libraries, school libraries, research libraries, and libraries that service specific needs, such as corporate, law, and medical libraries. The particular language skills required will also depend upon what specific area you work in within the library organization.

Understanding your attitudes toward your work environment is very important when considering a job in library service. Library types are defined by the community that they are designed to serve. Within the library profession, there are ample opportunities for both technically minded and people-oriented personalities. Corporate and research libraries are highly structured, and the information needs of their users are often very technical and demanding. The parameters are highly specific and detailed and may come with deadlines and cost restraints. School and public libraries, on the other hand, are far less demanding of technical skills but require a more people-centered approach.

In all types of libraries and all facets of the job, computers are playing a larger role. Anyone contemplating a career in library service or information science needs to be comfortable with computers and other information technologies. Because of the rapid advances and upgrades in this industry, you must also be adaptable and trainable. A technical understanding of computers is not necessary, just a familiarity with computer applications and a willingness to learn more. How your language skills can help you, and what expertise is required on the job, is more precisely determined by the area of the library you work in, by the opportunities that arise, and by the effort you expend.

Training

Whatever job you perform in the library world, it is important to get training in library skills and information management. It's always a good idea to get volunteer or entry-level experience on the job to see if you like the work and to acquire basic knowledge. Many colleges and universities offer elective courses in library use and bibliographic instruction that can be very valuable. High-level jobs and employment at research libraries generally require a master's degree in library and information science.

All library jobs fall into one of two categories: patron services or technical services. Those in the first category work directly with the community, and the key responsibility is reference service.

Patron Services

Reference librarians deal directly with library users and help patrons locate the information they desire. In public and school libraries, this requires good human relations skills. Technical perfection in a second language is not as important as being open to foreign language patrons at the library and understanding their needs. Basic conversational skills are paramount, and developing basic reading skills in another language enables a librarian to find the appropriate book or magazine for a patron—even if the vocabulary of the material itself is beyond the librarian's capabilities. Here, too, a feeling for the culture beyond words and verb conjugations is a valuable asset.

Many libraries seek to expand their offerings to include titles in the native languages of their clients. Chris, a librarian in an inner-city grade school, calls Spanish-speaking people in the area for leads on books written in Spanish that children enjoy. She also attends book fairs to get ideas and occasionally visits a Spanish-speaking country on a book-buying tour.

Library administrators are looking for confident, open employees to staff their reference departments—employees who are comfortable with people regardless of their ethnic or language backgrounds. If you are a people person who is willing to use your language skills—however halting and rudimentary—to communicate with patrons and successfully help them find the library materials they seek, you will be a valuable addition to a public or school library staff.

Reference work at a research or corporate/special library requires a much greater fluency in foreign languages and higher-level research skills. Where the information sought at a public library may consist of a good book or a consumer report on used cars, the information needs at research and special libraries are usually far more technical and exacting. A broad vocabulary in all your acquired languages is a must in order to understand patron queries and provide accurate answers.

If working in reference or in special libraries interests you, plan on extensive educational preparation. In university research libraries, it is routine to require one or even two foreign language proficiencies for a reference position. In addition, an advanced degree in library science and a college degree in the specific subject within which you will work is required. Your undergraduate work should include developing an understanding of the technical vocabulary within your subject specialty.

Your chosen subject specialty will often dictate the language proficiency that would be most useful. Any foreign language fluency can be useful, but for some specialties certain languages are more helpful than others. For example, if you have a bachelor's degree in chemistry and wish to work as a science or reference librarian, German, Russian, and Japanese would be more useful to you than Polish or Portuguese. If you work in literature or economics, Spanish, French, or Chinese might be more applicable than Bahasa Indonesian. On the other hand, if the library caters to a community of Portuguese- or Indonesian-speaking people, then these would be the most useful languages.

Because reference librarians at these larger or more specialized libraries can also be asked to translate material for patrons, the most advanced language proficiencies can make you very useful and valuable. Translating articles or technical manuals within a research discipline requires the most fluency and technical skills of any library language assignment.

Technical Services

The second category of library work is technical services. Here, librarians work with the information materials directly—whether they are books, paintings, movies, exhibits, or electronic data. They work to categorize, catalog, and organize the materials to make them readily available and accessible to the community. These jobs do not require the interpersonal communication skills that jobs in patron services do. As in reference, different levels of language ability can be useful in the technical services area.

Acquisitions

Acquisition of material is an important technical service. This department selects material for purchase. Prescreening of foreign language material may only require a rudimentary understanding of another language, enough to make the librarian capable of recognizing a good review in a literary publication in that language. When materials arrive in the library, someone must decide what department should receive them. This is not simple, particularly in the case of materials published or produced in a foreign country. Research libraries, in particular, receive materials from all over the world and not just materials that support the teaching of foreign languages. In assembling a reliable collection on any subject, there are important contributions made in many languages. When this material arrives at the library, someone needs to identify what language it is in and what subject area it deals with, which requires a broad familiarity with languages rather than fluency.

Materials in foreign languages purchased by public or school libraries are not as far ranging. Foreign language needs are dictated by the community the library serves. It is important for employees to have language skills that reflect the demographics of the local community. In the United States, the single most important second language for a public or school librarian is Spanish. In Eastern Canada it is French. In most urban areas, any second language skill will be valuable.

Cataloging

The second major technical service is cataloging. To be a cataloger in a research or special library requires an advanced degree in library science, as well as a high level of language expertise. Catalogers must identify the key subjects addressed by the material and then accurately describe it both in the principal language of the library in which it appears and in English. This requires a broad vocabulary, since, like reference service researchers, library catalogers usually specialize in one or more subject areas. This means they must have the expanded vocabulary requisite for their specializations. Though technical accuracy is a must, verbal communication skills are not necessary. All of a cataloger's job is reading and writing, so proper accents and vocal nuance are unnecessary.

If you are interested in being a part of the information age and have a bit of the private-eye spirit in you, your second language or multilingual skills can be put to profitable use in library and information science. If you like to find the needle in the haystack—the *Stecknadel* in the *Hauhaufen*, the *aguja* in the *pajar*, and the *tsahts'–s'* in the *tl'oh*—this could be the job for you.

Opportunities and Rewards

Job opportunities are expected to be very good for librarians even though job growth will be relatively slow. That's because a large number of librarians are expected to retire in the coming decade. According to the *Occupational Outlook Handbook*, employment of library assistants and library technicians is expected to grow as fast as the average for all occupations through 2014. With changing roles within libraries, library assistants and technicians are taking on more responsibility.

Salaries for librarians are highest in university and college libraries—around $47,000 a year. Salaries for elementary and primary school librarians were around $44,000, while local government librarians were paid $40,000. Salaries for library technicians in the categories of libraries cited ranged from $23,000 to $30,000 a year. Most library assistants were paid $11 to $15 an hour in 2007.

For More Information

Employers often list jobs with schools in their geographical areas. Newspapers can be another good resource. The *New York Times* Sunday "Week in Review" carries a special section of ads for librarian jobs in addition to the regular classifieds. Other large city newspapers often carry job vacancy listings for libraries, both professional and paraprofessional.

A list of accredited library and information studies programs can be requested from the American Library Association or found on its website. For more information, contact:

American Library Association
50 East Huron Street
Chicago, IL 60611
www.ala.org

Other organizations that offer career information in library and information science include:

American Society for Information Science and Technology
1320 Fenwick Lane, Suite 510
Silver Spring, MD 20910
www.asis.org

Canadian Library Association
328 Frank Street
Ottawa, ON K2P 0X8
Canada
www.cla.ca

Special Libraries Association
331 South Patrick Street
Alexandria, VA 22314
www.sla.org

CHAPTER SIX

Health Care

A front-page headline in *USA Today* on July 20, 2006, said it all: "Language barriers plague hospitals; Study: Patients are put at risk." The news story began, "Many hospital patients who have a limited ability to speak English and who need a translator don't get one, which puts them at risk for poor and sometimes life-threatening medical care." These language problems are greatly reduced when medical personnel speak the predominant foreign language needed in a medical clinic or hospital setting.

As Stefani, a family physician, prepares for work each morning, she knows two things will happen during her shift: she and her colleagues will be very busy, and much of the time she won't be speaking English. Stefani is a doctor at an inner-city medical clinic located in the Intermountain West, where 80 to 90 percent of her patients are native speakers of Spanish. Fortunately, as Stefani worked hard to become a good physician, she also worked hard to become bilingual. Before medical school, she studied abroad in Spain. During medical training, Stefani trained with medical doctors in Bolivia and Cuba.

Categories

There are two broad job categories within health care: health diagnostic occupations and health assessment and treatment occupations. Health diagnostic occupations include these job titles:

Chiropractor
Dentist

Ophthalmologist
Optometrist
Physician
Podiatrist
Orthopedist

Health assessment and treatment occupations include these professionals:

Dietitian and nutritionist
Radiologist
Occupational therapist
Psychiatrist
Pharmacist
Physical therapist
Physician assistant
Recreational therapist
Registered nurse
Respiratory therapist
Speech-language pathologist and audiologist

Knowledge of other languages is a distinct asset in all of these occupations. Most health workers deal directly with people, and because increasing numbers of people needing health services in the United States have a primary language other than English, the need for multilingual people in the health professions is very high. In addition, many medical-related tasks require people who work behind the scenes to use foreign language skills to help people get healthy and stay healthy.

Following is a list of jobs and positions in health care not mentioned in previous lists:

Dental assistant
Dental hygienist

Dietary aide
Emergency medical technician
Hospital care investigator
Licensed practical nurse
Paramedic

. . . .

Requirements

Before you investigate specific jobs, you should consider your atti-tude toward the health profession. Would you enjoy working with people who have health or emotional problems? Do you have the type of personality that would make you able to work in an atmosphere where conditions are often hectic and demand a com-bination of tact and decisiveness?

All of these professions require special training. The health diagnostic occupations require medical degrees. Four to six years of college—plus many hours of practicum—is generally the min-imum level of training required for the health assessment and treatment occupations.

There are, however, some health-related occupations that require much less training. You may want to work in one of these jobs to get a better sense of health-related work before you invest in the many years of training that many of the health occupations require. Some of these jobs are highlighted next.

. . . .

Job Descriptions

If you are interested in a health care position, then the next step is to investigate the opportunities that are available for you to use language skills that you have, or that you may develop, in health care jobs.

Here are some job descriptions in the health field for you to consider.

Ambulatory Care Technician

People in hospitals, clinics, assisted-living facilities, and nursing homes who are unable to move around completely on their own require technicians to help. When people can't walk and have trouble making their needs known because of language barriers, their frustration levels rise. Your training in a foreign language, even if it is minimal, could help these people move around and communicate.

Biomedical Equipment Technician

More and more machines and instruments are being developed to test people and assist them with various kinds of ailments. People who operate these biomedical machines must be trained technicians. They must also have people skills because patients undergoing medical testing are often nervous and upset. If you can explain biomedical procedures quietly and effectively in the language with which the patient is most comfortable, you will help the whole team that is trying to make that person well.

Mental Health Assistant

Although mental health assistants don't work with instruments and machines the way biomedical technicians do, they still need specialized training. With the increasing stress of modern society and the high incidence of drug- and alcohol-related illnesses, there is a growing need for mental health assistants with skills in psychology and human behavior. If people have emotional problems and also are unable to communicate to mental health workers because of language difficulties, the situation is obviously very serious. You can use mental health training and your language skills to help such people and develop a very rewarding career in the mental health profession.

Medical Records Clerk

You may be attracted to the health profession, but working directly with people may not be what you do best. That's fine, because there are jobs in the health field where you can contribute without dealing directly with patients. All health problems need to be documented. With the vast number of immigrants, tourists, and foreign visitors to the United States, there is a need for multi-lingual record keepers. You may find it rewarding to use your language skills in helping health care professionals translate health documents and health insurance forms into English.

Allied Health Professionals

This group of health care professionals includes respiratory, occupational, and physical therapists; radiology (x-ray) technicians; medical technologists; and phlebotomists (those who draw blood). All of these professions involve patient contact and involve doing medical procedures that can be stressful and painful. Any second language skills can be invaluable in alleviating trauma for the patient. Speaking the patient's native language enables the health care professional to do a better job, resulting in better medical care.

Patients who are able to communicate with their health care givers and to clearly understand what is being done to them, and why it is being done, are better able to cooperate and are less anxious about their treatment. As a health care worker, it is also extremely beneficial to be able to explain the procedure to the patient's family or friends. A second language skill that facilitates such communication can greatly ease the anxiety associated with health care.

Licensed Practical Nurse and Nurse's Aide

This group of health care workers has by far the greatest amount of patient contact. Nurses who have language skills that enable them to talk with their patients and receive feedback from patients are able to give the best possible care and experience the best possible results.

Nurses also have the most interaction with the patient's family and friends, and clear communication with them can be crucial in establishing a medical history and in relieving anxiety and stress in both the patients and their loved ones. The nurse or aide often serves as a go-between for the patient and the physician. Therefore, the clearer the clinical picture the nurse is able to obtain, the better the treatment the whole health care team can provide.

Emergency Medical Technician (EMT)

These people respond to all sorts of emergencies. A second language ability that reflects the demographics of the area where they work can be a crucial, perhaps even life-saving, skill for EMTs. Since they must respond to emergency calls, EMTs are not always able to predict the language of the patient. Often the patient is unconscious, and in such cases communication with the family or witnesses of the situation can be vital to the success of treatment. This can be a very stressful occupation but also a very rewarding one that offers an opportunity to use many skills, including second language capabilities.

Home Health Aides

Home health aides help people who have had health or emotional problems and now need home visits from time to time to monitor their progress and give them assistance. Understanding the client's language and having an appreciation for the client's culture is essential in providing good health care.

For example, a sizable community of people from the Dominican Republic resides in a town in New Jersey. When what most temperate-zone Americans would regard as minor changes in temperature occur, many Dominicans feel a cold coming on. To help them feel comfortable in their new homes, one successful home health aide provided them with an orientation that included how to identify cod liver oil and where to buy it. In syrup or pill form, cod liver oil is widely taken in many parts of Latin America as a cough remedy.

Opportunities and Rewards

Health care is one of the fastest-growing and most human-resource-intensive industries in the United States and abroad. The U.S. Bureau of Labor Statistics reports that one out of every five new jobs created by 2014 will be in the health services field. The *Occupational Outlook Handbook* says employment of medical and health services managers is expected to grow faster than the average for all occupations through 2014 as the health care industry continues to expand and diversify. Job opportunities will be especially good in offices of health practitioners, general medical and surgical hospitals, home health care services, and outpatient care centers.

Wages and salaries for health care jobs range from minimum wage for some positions requiring no training to the stratosphere (for some doctors and researchers). To give one example, median annual earnings of medical and health services managers was around $70,000 in 2007.

For More Information

The following organizations should be helpful in gathering further information on health care careers. It is always a good idea to include a self-addressed, stamped envelope with your request.

Aboriginal Nurses Association of Canada
56 Sparks Street, Suite 502
Ottawa, ON K1P 5A9
Canada
www.anac.on.ca

American Academy of Physician Assistants (AAPA)
950 North Washington Street
Alexandria, VA 22314
www.aapa.org

American Association for Respiratory Care
9425 North MacArthur Boulevard, Suite 100
Irving, TX 75063
www.aarc.org

American Association of Colleges of Osteopathic Medicine
(AACOM)
5550 Friendship Boulevard, Suite 310
Chevy Chase, MD 20815
www.aacom.org

American Dental Education Association (ADEA)
1400 K Street NW, Suite 1100
Washington, DC 20005
www.adea.org

American Medical Association (AMA)
515 North State Street
Chicago, IL 60610
www.ama-assn.org

American Nurses Association (ANA)
815 Georgia Avenue, Suite 400
Silver Spring, MD 20910
www.nursingworld.org

American Occupational Therapy Association (AOTA)
4720 Montgomery Lane
PO Box 31220
Bethesda, MD 20824
www.aota.org

American Optometric Association (AOA)
243 North Lindbergh Boulevard
St. Louis, MO 63141
www.aoa.org

American Physical Therapy Association (APTA)
1111 North Fairfax Street
Alexandria, VA 22314
www.apta.org

American Society of Health-System Pharmacists
7272 Wisconsin Avenue
Bethesda, MD 20814
www.ashp.org

American Speech-Language-Hearing Association (ASHA)
10801 Rockville Pike
Rockville, MD 20852
www.asha.org

Association of American Medical Colleges (AAMC)
2450 N Street NW
Washington, DC 20037
www.aamc.org

Association of Schools and Colleges of Optometry (ASCO)
6110 Executive Boulevard, Suite 420
Rockville, MD 20852
www.opted.org

Canadian Association of Critical Care Nurses
PO Box 25322
London, ON N6C 6B1
Canada
www.caccn.ca/about.htm

Canadian Dental Association
1815 Alta Vista Drive
Ottawa, ON K1G 3Y6
Canada
www.cda-adc.ca

Canadian Institute for Health Information (CIHI)
495 Richmond Road, Suite 600
Ottawa, ON K2A 4H6
Canada
www.cihi.ca

Canadian Nurses Association (CNA)
50 Driveway
Ottawa, ON K2P 1E2
Canada
www.cna-nurses.ca

Canadian Physiotherapy Association
2345 Yonge Street, Suite 410
Toronto, ON M4P 2E5
Canada
www.physiotherapy.ca

Canadian Osteopathic and Medical Association
110-4935 Fortieth Avenue NW
Calgary, AB T3A 2N1
Canada
www.osteopathic.ca

International Chiropractors Association (ICA)
1110 North Glebe Road, Suite 650
Arlington, VA 22201
www.chiropractic.org

National League for Nursing (NLN)
61 Broadway, Thirty-Third Floor
New York, NY 10006
www.nln.org

National Student Nurses' Association (NSNA)
45 Main Street, Suite 606
Brooklyn, NY 11201
www.nsna.org

National Therapeutic Recreation Society (NTRS)
(affiliated with National Recreation and Park Association)
22377 Belmont Ridge Road
Ashburn, VA 20148
www.nrpa.org (search for NTRS)

Volunteer Organizations

Following are some organizations that need health care professionals with foreign language skills.

American Friends Service Committee
1501 Cherry Street
Philadelphia, PA 19102
www.afsc.org

American Red Cross National Headquarters
2025 E Street NW
Washington, DC 20006
www.redcross.org

CARE
650 First Avenue, Second Floor
New York, NY 10016
www.care.org

Doctors Without Borders
333 Seventh Avenue, Second Floor
New York, NY 10001
www.doctorswithoutborders.org

MercyCorps
Department W
PO Box 2669
Portland, OR 97208
www.mercycorps.org

World Health Organization (WHO)
Avenue Appia 20
CH 1211 Geneva 27
Switzerland
www.who.int

CHAPTER SEVEN

Human Services

Paul was a social services caseworker in a rural area of Eastern Kansas. He felt fortunate that he spoke some Spanish and was cross-culturally adept because his caseload included Hispanic families and people with a variety of ethnic backgrounds. Paul's daily work was as varied as the people he served. He dealt with mental health issues, substance-abuse problems, truant school-children, domestic violence, community outreach projects, and much more.

The field of human services is an interesting professional area with employment opportunities for people with language skills. Like health care professionals, human services workers come into contact with people who are poor, unemployed, homeless, victims of abuse, or in poor health. The work settings include group homes and halfway houses; correctional centers; mental health facilities; family, child, and youth service agencies; and substance-abuse treatment centers.

As society becomes more diverse, many human services clients will speak languages other than English as their native tongue, which will make it easier for qualified people with language skills to find jobs in the field of human services.

The huge increase in the immigrant population is also a source of jobs in private and government organizations that help immigrants and other people with limited fluency in English get along in the United States and Canada. These groups require employment counselors, caseworkers, and supervisors who speak the languages of their clients. Opportunities for human service careers are not limited to major cities, where immigrant populations tend to be large. Many immigrant people live in widely dispersed areas of the country. They are found in all regions and states, in big cities and small towns.

There are positions in social work that involve working with employment records, resumes, legal documents of all kinds, and correspondence with social agencies abroad. This work requires people who are able to decipher foreign languages and elicit information from unfamiliar documents.

Job Requirements and Challenges

As with positions in the health care professions, human services positions tend to be people intensive. They require you to be interested in helping others with a variety of social needs, from education and employment to individual personal and family matters. If your career plan includes some kind of human services, study the ways in which language skills and human skills combine in this area. You will want to focus your efforts on what will make things better for your clients.

You should familiarize yourself with the regulations and requirements of the social agencies and organizations you represent. You will want to identify potential problems that these regulations and requirements might pose for clients who speak a language other than English and who may come from a cultural background different from your own. As a human services worker, you might encounter cross-cultural challenges. Such potential problems may not lie just in the differences in language. If people have religious, dietary, social, or political customs or beliefs that conflict with the regulations of your agency or organization, you may be the only person who can solve the dilemma. And to solve it, you will have to understand the regulations involved as well as the cultural reality that controls your client.

One example of a cultural tradition clashing with the tradition of a social service agency occurred in Chicago when a state agency attempted to provide group health and education counseling to a tribe of Roma (Gypsies). The way the agency organized the group sessions offended these Gypsies' sense of propriety. The agency had proposed that the groups be divided into age levels. The Gypsy leaders were horrified that grandchildren were to be separated from their grandparents and equally upset that males and females were to be together in the same class. The counselors in this case proved to be flexible, and a simple compromise solution was agreed upon—to divide the classes by sex but not by age. Social service work often demands the ability to make such compromises.

Social Work

Social workers generally help people who are having difficulties dealing with circumstances in their lives. There are many kinds of social workers. The major areas of social work include child welfare and family services, mental health, medical social work, school social work, planning and policy development, and social welfare administration. A bachelor's degree is usually the minimum academic requirement to work in these fields. Often a master's degree is required. A social worker's effectiveness in helping people who do not speak English is greatly aided by a knowledge of the client's native tongue.

Frequently, the needs of someone from a particular country can be anticipated by a knowledge of the client's culture. Many people from India, for instance, are Hindu. Among their religious practices is a proscription against eating meat. It would be helpful, therefore, to be able to identify area restaurants where good vegetarian food is served—not just fruit salads.

Community Affairs

There are many levels of positions and opportunities in community affairs planning and community affairs communication. They range from planning a single activity to setting up and carrying out community activities to bearing overall responsibility for planning and coordinating all cultural and linguistic efforts that a community undertakes.

Planning

If you have organizational skills, you may want to work with people who plan activities that focus on, or seek participation of, ethnic and linguistic groups in the community. These activities may be anything from a large-budget annual observance, such as Spanish-American Heritage Week, which is put on for the whole community or region, to a picnic for preschool children in a small ethnic neighborhood.

It is difficult to overemphasize the need for knowledge of the cultures involved as well as sensitivity to the social hierarchy of the target community. You may have to check with people about what colors to use in banners and bunting, what sort of food and drink would be appropriate, and which dates to plan events and which dates to avoid holding certain activities. Advice on the type and location of sites for the events may also be needed.

Communication

This work involves, among other things, getting the English-language mass media—newspapers, magazines, radio, and television—to be aware of, and involved with, the cultural and linguistic groups in your community. It also involves writing, public speaking, and identifying other individuals in the target community who are good spokespersons.

Sometimes it is difficult to find any long-term residents of a community who speak the language of the most recent residents. There are towns in Minnesota, for example, that have become home to sizable numbers of Hmong immigrants, a mountain tribe of farmers from Southeast Asia. Making effective contact with them has required identifying a network of human resources in the state to help inform social workers about Hmong customs, aspirations, and problems. People who could speak Hmong were needed to assist in the initial contacts. One successful community affairs planner not only set up a good network of people who could contribute something to the needs of the Hmong; he also made arrangements to have local Hmong tutor him in the language. This was widely appreciated in the Hmong community.

Opportunities and Rewards

Job opportunities in human services are expected to be excellent, particularly for applicants with appropriate postsecondary education. The number of human service jobs are projected to grow much faster than the average for all occupations between 2004 and 2014—ranking the occupation among the most rapidly growing.

Jobs for social workers in private and government agencies have increased markedly in the last half-dozen years as changes in the welfare system have promoted more aggressive public and private sector actions to deal with welfare recipients. Salaries for these jobs are also on the rise, according to organizations that monitor this sector of the nation's workforce. The job outlook calls for a faster-than-average expansion in the number of jobs available through the year 2010. One area of growth, for example, is in services to the aging. Baby boomers—people born between 1946 and 1964—are retiring. This huge sector of the nation's population will seek more social services as they age.

In 2007, earnings for social and human services assistants, for example, ranged from $29,000 a year for state employees to $21,000 for those working in residential mental retardation, mental health, and substance-abuse facilities. Managers and people with specialized training earned considerably more.

For More Information

Further information on job openings in the field of human services may be available from state or provincial employment agencies or from city, county, state, or provincial departments of health, mental health, and human resources.

Additional information is available from the following:

Center for Multicultural Human Services
701 West Broad Street, Suite 305
Falls Church, VA 22046
www.cmhsweb.org

Council for Standards in Human Service Education
PMB 703
1050 Larrabee Avenue, Suite 104
Bellingham, WA 98225
www.cshse.org

Human Resources and Social Development Canada
www.hrsdc.gc.ca

National Multicultural Institute
3000 Connecticut Avenue NW, Suite 438
Washington, DC 20008
www.nmci.org

National Organization for Human Services
90 Madison Street, Suite 206
Denver, CO 80206
www.nationalhumanservices.org

CHAPTER EIGHT

Journalism and Mass Communication

I t's a weird and wonderful world out there in media land, and because it is, people with language skills are finding all kinds of new career opportunities.

The Changing Media Landscape

Powerful forces have transformed the media of mass communication and the practice of journalism in recent years. Giant conglomerates have bought whole mass media industries and consolidated them. By 2007 conglomerates owned more than 90 percent of the media market. These conglomerates function in every field of mass media, from huge movie, music, and entertainment companies to small-town radio stations and newspapers. Consolidation has transformed the way journalists and other mass media practitioners work. Journalism education programs teach aspiring newspaper reporters to shoot video. Students who say they want to go into advertising are taught to report for print media and write blogs. It's called convergence communication.

Media and communications industries are still good places to look for jobs and career opportunities because there have been huge increases in job categories and career choices. Another plus is that media and communication industries have gone global and their hiring practices reflect the need for workers with foreign language and cross-cultural skills. Opportunities for self-employed media specialists have also grown enormously with the technological developments and the expansion of the World Wide Web.

The Internet has created a need for people with skills in writing, video, animation, illustration, photography, and music. The people who write, animate, illustrate, and take photographs have to be managed. People who can manage visual, technical, creative, economic, and political transactions, many happening in real time, in cross-cultural settings, are greatly in demand.

The options and opportunities are so numerous and varied that the best advice is to log on and look up the resources you need to move ahead with job and media career possibilities. The information revolution of the late twentieth century gave labels to career paths and jobs in communications and media. Many of these jobs are still around but with new names and job profiles. Newspapers and magazines are still delivered to your door, but they are also available online. Jobs for word people may be listed under labels such as information architecture, multimedia journalism, online media sales, corporate communications, community communications, training and development, and account relations.

Early in the computer age, most typewriter companies saw themselves as manufacturers of machines. IBM saw itself as a word-processing organization. When typewriters and the companies that made them went the way of buggy whips, words were still being processed abundantly at IBM. The new environment simply shifts the focus from the single medium to multilevel, multimedia communication. Arthur Sulzberger Jr., publisher of the *New York Times,* put it this way: "I don't give a tinker's damn how we distribute our information. . . . I'll be pleased to beam it directly to your cortex." Sometime in the future, the *New York Times* will cease to be produced on newsprint by roaring presses, but you can bet that the *Times* organization will still be in the information distribution business.

You should think of yourself in terms of the skills you possess and not how well you might fit a specific job description. You can tailor your skills and capabilities to fit the career path you choose.

As you consider a career in communication, remember that multinational media companies are developing and marketing vast numbers of media products abroad, and they want the people who represent them to speak more than one language and to be able to think and act effectively in cross-cultural situations.

Print Media

Until the world switches entirely to electronic information technology, you'll still find a wide range of job opportunities within traditional print media organizations, including book, magazine, and newspaper publishers. To these have been added online books, e-zines, and online newspapers.

Book Publishing

Thousands of new books are published each year. Take a look at any traditional or online bookstore and see for yourself. And nearly as many will be translated for markets overseas or translated into English for the U.S. market. Publishers need a variety of people in a number of positions to read and translate manuscripts. Here are some of the jobs in book publishing today:

Acquisitions editor
Audio book abridger
Author
Blog coordinator
Book buyer
Book marketer
Book packager
Book reviewer
Copyeditor
Editor
Editorial assistant
Freelance writer
Graphic designer

Online sales director
Proofreader
Publisher
Translator

The job opportunities in book publishing are diverse. Books are beginning to be published directly on the Internet, as well, which involves additional skills. Most jobs require a combination of language skills and some other talent, such as artistic, sales, or writing ability. If publishing interests you, plan to develop both your language skills and another specialization. For example, designers need a background in art, and promoters often study marketing. And many publishing professionals take continuing education courses designed specifically for those in the field.

As in all fields, work experience is the best way to test your interest and aptitude. Internships, entry-level jobs, and freelance positions provide great on-the-job training and a good introduction to the world of publishing. You can locate potential employers through numerous search engines on the Internet and through the reference desk at your local library.

Magazines

Magazines originally developed from newspapers but have since nearly swamped the publishing world. Using better paper, more color and photographs, and a different writing style, magazines have constantly evolved to suit the needs and whims of society. Now, specialty magazines cover every conceivable subject, from cats to monster movies, from log homes to modern science. And many specialty magazines have begun to serve the needs of people with a second language.

Here are some common positions on a magazine staff:

Acquisitions editor
Art director
Circulation/subscription manager

Columnist
Contributing editor
Copyeditor
Design and layout editor
Editorial assistant
Freelance writer
Illustrator
Online magazine editor
Photographer
Proofreader
Researcher
Staff writer

Because magazines offer diverse job options and cover a wide range of subjects, you should be able to combine your skills and interests in seeking a job in this field. Jobs for editors and graphic artists have increased dramatically. Competition for jobs in magazine and book publishing is stiff. However, skill in a second language can help make you more marketable.

You should plan to combine your language skills with other specialized education and as much job experience as you can develop before seeking your first full-time job in publishing. Major cities such as New York and Chicago are headquarters to many magazines, but technology has made it possible for staffers to work at home or in distant offices.

Newspapers

Major consolidations and market pressures led to the demise of the Knight-Ridder publishing group in 2006. The high cost of paper and printing may yet lead to dramatic changes in the way news is disseminated, but the newspaper industry isn't going to disappear anytime soon.

Many of the jobs at newspapers are similar to those at magazines or publishing houses. The main differences between newspaper and magazine work are writing styles and content.

Newspapers generally focus on timely newsworthy events, possibly going into depth on a topic over a period of several days of daily publishing. Magazines, by their nature, have longer deadline periods that allow the writer more time to dig into a story, develop it, and deliver it in a polished form.

Newspapers have access to the worldwide news-gathering capabilities of the Associated Press as well as foreign news services such as Reuters and Agence France-Presse. Nevertheless, when important news breaks abroad, newspapers may send their own staff reporters to the scene. This is particularly true when the news event affects the local area directly.

Staff reporters chosen for these short-term overseas assignments are, first, good reporters. Second, they are often persons with language or cross-cultural skills. Often the language the reporter speaks may not be the language of the area where the news event is taking place, but local editors often perceive individuals with language skills as qualified for assignments anywhere abroad.

In addition to using language skills abroad, local reporters use their target languages in their daily assignments. Newspapers are putting a much greater emphasis than ever before on broadly representing the people in their circulation areas in their news reports and feature stories. Often this involves interviewing people with little or no fluency in English. The number of bilingual newspapers, both printed and electronic, is growing.

The increase of online editions to virtually all daily newspapers has created more jobs. Creation of positions for graphic designers, Web masters, and circulation sales and promotion personnel, among many others, has widened the field of jobs available in the newspaper industry. The increasing number of small-town and suburban papers, combined with the high turnover rate in the industry, will provide new jobs for journalism graduates. And language skills will give you a competitive edge, especially if they are combined with a degree in journalism and experience on your school or local paper.

Opportunities and Rewards

According to the *Occupational Outlook Handbook*, competition will continue to be keen for jobs on large metropolitan and national newspapers and magazines. Most job opportunities will be with small-town and suburban newspapers. Talented writers who can handle foreign languages or highly specialized scientific or technical subjects have an advantage. Also, newspapers increasingly are hiring freelancers. Salaries for news analysts, reporters, and correspondents vary widely. Median annual earnings of reporters and correspondents were around $33,000 in 2007. The middle 50 percent earned between $23,000 and $50,000. The lowest 10 percent earned less than $18,470.

Electronic Media

Three technologies of the nineteenth century—the telegraph, the telephone, and the radio—prepared the way for the media that were to follow: sound recording, motion pictures, television, computers, and the Internet.

Radio

Radio has changed dramatically over the decades. It began as a medium of the spoken word, became a medium of sophisticated entertainment programs—including comedy, drama, game, and variety shows—then was gradually overshadowed by the rising star of television.

Formats changed, listeners changed, but radio continued to grow. The introduction of satellite transmissions with listeners who pay monthly fees to receive scores of channels brought a whole new dimension to radio. What car on the road is complete without a radio? What home doesn't have a radio in every bedroom? All oldies, all rock, all gospel, all talk, all news—all these formats are flourishing across the nation.

Talk radio has become the fastest-growing format in radio; millions of American adults listen to an hour of talk radio a week.

One of the most dramatic changes in radio came in 2000, when the Federal Communications Commission (FCC) announced that it was setting up hundreds of free, low-power radio stations for nonprofit groups across the country. The FCC wanted to increase the diversity of voices on the airwaves. In 2006, the Senate Commerce Committee voted to expand low-power FM radio as an amendment to a large telecommunication bill that covered everything from public access to the Internet to public-access TV stations. In June 2006, Senators John McCain and Patrick Leahy introduced a measure that supported the introduction of hundreds of community radio stations that can reach listeners up to 3.5 miles away. New legislation favoring low-power neighborhood FM radio stations could be the biggest change in the radio industry since the growth of FM in the 1960s. Many of these stations beam their broadcasts to foreign language listeners.

On the other end of the radio spectrum, the FCC changed some of its policies that limited commercial station ownership. The FCC now allows cross-media ownership in the same market. Before the change, the FCC would not grant broadcast licenses to owners of newspapers in the same city.

Spanish broadcast stations are common all over the United States, and the government still beams foreign language programming into hundreds of countries. Jobs abound in radio for people with second languages. Although the skill generally is not required for employment, in most cases there are those positions for which a second language is a prerequisite.

Here are some of the jobs you could pursue:

Advertising manager
Business development director
Commercial station manager
Engineer
Local/national/international sales representative
News announcer
News reporter/writer

Producer
Promotions director
Public service director
Station manager
Talk show host
Traffic/continuity manager

Television

Public television is the most powerful mass communication medium in the world—it combines near-universal and instantaneous delivery of sound, sight, and motion at no cost to the viewer. And television delivers local as well as national and international content. Broadcast television in the United States is currently a mass medium whose success depends on delivering a hundred million or so households to advertisers of products everyone uses. In Canada, though the market is much smaller, the same advertising dynamics apply. But cable, computers, fiber optics, and the Internet give consumers much more control over what they view.

Major manufacturers of home entertainment and information products offer receivers that deliver digital-quality audio-video and instant software downloads to personal computers. Such networks can deliver customized media information and entertainment to the desktop computer via digital TV broadcasting, thus combining the efficiency and immediacy of broadcast with the customization and control of the home computer.

The need for program content is enormous. The flow of programming between nations rose as European and Asian nations produced their own giant conglomerates to compete with those in the United States and Canada. The growth and development of television means jobs at home and abroad at all levels of the industry. The array of jobs in television includes:

Broadcast analyst
Graphic artist

News announcer
News director
Producer
Program director
Promotions director
Sales personnel
Station manager
Technical engineer
Technical director
Videotape and digital editor
Website director

As you would imagine, most of these jobs require specialized skills and training unrelated to foreign language fluency. However, as the number of Spanish language and educational stations increases, fluency in a second language will be a special asset in this competitive field.

Foreign Correspondents

The largest and most affluent news organizations have overseas bureaus staffed by foreign correspondents. The reporters who work for these prestigious organizations are among the best reporters in the world. Back home, highly trained, often linguistically and cross-culturally trained editors receive their material. Executives of these organizations, if asked, say that their overseas bureaus are staffed exclusively by individuals who worked their way up from news operations. Because the number of media with established foreign bureaus is limited, and it may take a good reporter a decade to get abroad, many people are dissuaded from aspiring to a career in foreign correspondence.

They needn't be. There is another way to become a foreign correspondent: going abroad as a freelancer. Anderson Cooper did that. He took a video camera overseas and began covering news. He sold his work to television news organizations. He became the anchor of CNN's highly regarded nightly news show "Anderson

Cooper 360°." Freelance correspondents work for themselves anywhere in the world. They sell news and feature material in all formats—print, electronic, and digital to news organizations in the United States.

In the stressful conditions that foreign correspondents often encounter, strong communication skills are a must. Not only are they important for your own comfort and safety, but such skills are an essential part of doing the job well. The correspondent's duty is to report the facts as completely and accurately as possible. In order to do that, a journalist must be able to understand his or her sources and the subtleties of the language they speak.

In addition, it is helpful for foreign correspondents to attain as much knowledge of and sensitivity to other cultures as they can. Such awareness often makes it easier for a journalist to gain the confidence of sources and hosts in another country. Understanding the culture is just part of the job.

Citizen Journalism

Technology has produced a news phenomenon that Microsoft chairman Bill Gates predicted would occur. As cell phones proliferated, citizen-driven communications—everyday people using video cameras and cell phones to record news as it breaks and publishing it on the Internet—swept the world. Some of the biggest news pictures of the decade, including the execution of Saddam Hussein, were citizen cell phone reports.

This kind of citizen journalism (also known as participatory journalism), according to a seminal report by media consultants Shayne Bowman and Chris Willis, can provide independent, reliable, accurate, wide-ranging, and relevant information that a democracy requires.

People with creativity and ingenuity can develop careers and jobs as cyberspace citizen journalists. Dan Gillmor is a proponent of citizen journalism. He founded the nonprofit Center for Citizen Media (www.citmedia.org), which is aimed at helping enable and encourage citizen journalism at every level. The Canadian

Broadcasting Corporation has started citizen media outlets on some of its French language stations. NowPublic.com, a citizen news startup based in Vancouver, British Columbia, posted citizens' images and news accounts on its website along with links to mainstream news organizations.

Opportunities and Rewards

Like the other communications careers, broadcasting is a popular field. It tends to attract more people than can find employment. The U.S. Department of Labor expects employment in broadcasting to increase 11 percent between 2004 and 2014. That's slower growth than the 14 percent projected for all industries combined.

When you're getting started, it is easiest to find a job with a smaller station, more than half of which employ fewer than ten people. The largest number of jobs overall are found in large establishments employing fifty or more people.

Competition will continue to be keen for jobs with large metropolitan and national broadcast stations and networks. Talented reporters who can handle highly specialized scientific or technical subjects will have the best opportunities. Salaries for broadcast news analysts, reporters, and correspondents vary widely. Median annual earnings for those job categories were around $35,000 in 2007. The lowest-paid earned around $22,000, while broadcasters in medium and large markets earned $70,000 or more.

For More Information

Agence France-Presse (AFP)
Paris - Headquarters
11-15 Place de la Bourse
75002 Paris
France
www.afp.com

American Federation of Television and Radio Artists (AFTRA)
New York National Office
260 Madison Avenue
New York, NY 10016
or
Los Angeles National Office
5757 Wilshire Boulevard, Ninth Floor
Los Angeles, CA 90036
www.aftra.org

American Society of Newspaper Editors
11690B Sunrise Valley Drive
Reston, VA 20191
www.asne.org

Associated Press Headquarters
450 West Thirty-Third Street
New York, NY 10001
www.ap.org

Associated Press Managing Editors
19 Commerce Court West
Cranbury, NJ 08512
www.apme.com

Newspaper Association of America
4401 Wilson Boulevard, Suite 900
Arlington, VA 22203
www.naa.org

Radio-Television News Directors Association/Foundation
   (RTNDA/RTNDF)
1600 K Street NW, Suite 700
Washington, DC 20006
www.rtndf.org

Reuters
The Reuters Building
South Colonnade
Canary Wharf
London E14 5EP
England

Society of Professional Journalists
Eugene S. Pulliam National Journalism Center
3909 North Meridian Street
Indianapolis, IN 46208
www.spj.org

CHAPTER NINE

The Entertainment Industry

The United States has exported entertainment and culture for more than a hundred years. From early silent movies to television series to jazz to handheld text-messaging devices, U.S. creativity and marketing have been the envy of competing countries. In recent years, mergers and buyouts of huge media companies have produced a phenomenon known as communication convergence. News, entertainment, and business organizations are welded together in conglomerates that promote each other's products while competing among themselves for consumer dollars. The creation of these huge corporations kept the United States competitive in the global marketplace in the first decade of the twenty-first century. Having the muscle to compete globally gave the United States the power to maintain its dominance as a producer of worldwide entertainment.

Until recently, U.S. entertainment entrepreneurs behaved culturally in the way nineteenth-century colonial powers had behaved politically—with little regard for the social, cultural, and linguistic implications of their actions. However, the U.S. cultural consciousness has risen significantly. Today the entertainment giants take all aspects of the global market into consideration. As a result, multilingual and cross-culturally trained individuals work at all levels in worldwide entertainment industries.

Entertainment produced for the masses still dominates entertainment products, from movies to television to music, but the industry is also home to thousands of niche markets. There's a place in this vast multilingual, multicultural arena for virtually anyone who has the stamina and determination to enter this fast-paced industry.

. . . .

Recorded Music

Record companies, often referred to as labels, make money by gaining control over a master recording of a performance by an artist and then selling copies to consumers. The acquisition of masters is referred to as the A & R (artist and repertoire) function. The function is easy to explain; the industry itself is more complex. Within individual labels or companies, the jobs are many and varied. There are far more than we can list here. Much more complete information is available on the Internet at sites such as www.musicians.about.com, but here are a few jobs of interest:

Artist relations representative
Bilingual rap artist
Business affairs specialist
Composer
Label president
Legal representative
Lyricist
Musician
Producer
Promoter
Public relations specialist
Recording engineer
Researcher
Salesperson
Studio musician
Talent agent
Technician
Vocalist

Movies

They don't call it the movie business for nothing. To understand the potential for jobs for foreign language aficionados in the motion picture industry, you have to think of movies as income-producing products. Movies were once shown exclusively in theaters. Now theater exhibition represents only a small portion of a movie's profit potential. A hit movie will begin at its first "window"—a movie theater in the United States or abroad. Then it appears in other windows of exhibition: video shops, pay-per-view television, cable television, network television, and syndicated television. Organizing and supervising this process is the work of thousands of people.

A critical task of anyone who supervises distribution of a product is to understand the receptiveness of customers—what do people want? What moves them? What excites them? At the front end of the process are the individuals who come up with ideas for movies that people will enjoy. They write them, script them, direct them, and produce them. Then there are those who distribute the movies. In both of these areas, cross-cultural and foreign language skills are increasingly sought after.

A career in motion pictures may mean work in any one of a dozen capacities. Here are a few of your options:

Animation artist
Casting director
Cinematographer
Director
Distribution specialist
Driver
Graphic artist
Makeup artist
Media liaison
On-screen talent
Photographer

Producer
Reviewer
Screenwriter
Script adapter
Set designer
Story analyst
Story editor
Stunt performer
Subsidiary rights agent

Creativity, Art, and Design

Do you possess a creative streak? Creative consultant Roger von Oech wrote about a large company that wanted to develop creativity among its research and design personnel. The company hired a team of psychologists to discover what made some employees more creative than others. What they found out was that the creative people thought they were creative and the less creative people didn't think they were. According to von Oech, the people who thought they were creative paid attention to their small ideas, played around with them, and built on them. The people who thought they weren't creative were generally too practical in their thinking.

Your mission, should you choose to accept it, is to admit to yourself and then state openly that you are a creative person and then work to prove it. Technology has provided you with unlimited opportunities to develop your creativity and play with your ideas. Add your cross-cultural and language capabilities to a belief in your own creativity, and you could be on the threshold of a great career. According to an essay by Ed Roberts in Albert N. Greco's *The Media and Entertainment Industries*, "A computer gives the average person, a high school freshman, the power to do things in a week that all the mathematicians who ever lived until thirty years ago couldn't do." The same could be said of the Internet in regard to artists, graphic designers, and creative people of all disciplines.

Here are some potential areas where jobs and career opportunities exist for those who admit they're creative:

Animation artist
Cartoonist
CD-ROM editor
Comic book writer
Creative consultant
Graphic designer
Electronic game designer
Illustrator
Video catalog editor
Video streaming specialist
Virtual reality designer
Web page master

Opportunities and Rewards

Wage and salary jobs in arts, entertainment, and recreation are projected to grow about 25 percent between 2007 and 2014, compared with 14 percent for all industries combined, according to the *Occupational Outlook Handbook*.

Rising incomes, leisure time, and awareness of the health benefits of physical fitness will increase the demand for arts, entertainment, and recreation services. Earnings in arts, entertainment, and recreation generally are low, reflecting the large number of part-time and seasonal jobs.

Nonsupervisory workers in arts, entertainment, and recreation averaged around $350 a week in 2007, compared with around $550 throughout private industry.

For More Information

For additional information on careers in the entertainment industry, contact the following associations:

Alliance of Canadian Cinema, Television, and Radio Artists
625 Church Street, Third Floor
Toronto, ON M4Y 2G1
Canada
www.actra.ca

American Federation of Television and Radio Artists (AFTRA)
260 Madison Avenue
New York, NY 10016
www.aftra.org

Broadcast Education Association
1771 N Street NW
Washington, DC 20036
www.beaweb.org

Radio-Television News Directors Association
1600 K Street NW, Suite 700
Washington, DC 20006
www.rtnda.org

Radio-Television News Directors Association Canada
2175 Sheppard Avenue East, Suite 310
Toronto, ON M2J 1W8
Canada
www.rtndacanada.com

CHAPTER TEN

Travel and Tourism

Travel and Tourism generates $1.3 trillion in economic activity in the United States every year. That equates to $3.5 billion a day, $148 million an hour, $2.4 million a minute, and $40,000 a second, according to the Travel Industry Association (TIA). The TIA reported that the travel and tourism industry is one of the country's largest employers, with 7.3 million travel-generated jobs, which means that one out of every eight U.S. nonfarm jobs is directly or indirectly created by travel and tourism. For its size and population, Canada has a similarly vigorous economic activity in travel and tourism.

Tourism and foreign travel continue to grow in the United States, but the common problem of poor communication, despite technological advances, remains a barrier in some areas of the travel industry. International travel agents indicated in a survey that language is one of the most serious problems in attracting foreign travelers to the United States. Former senator Paul Simon once quipped that the Immigration and Naturalization Service should erect a sign at our international airports: "Welcome to the United States. We do not speak your language."

Much progress has been made in the last fifteen years. The United States has many more language-qualified people in the travel and tourism industry than there were in the early 1990s. But there are still not enough to serve the vast numbers of foreign visitors who arrive each year. The travel and tourism industry needs language-qualified employees at all levels.

Whether it is for business or pleasure, travelers today require able, competent assistance with getting from one place to another. All of the associated businesses—such as car rentals, skycaps, luggage handling, reservation and ticket services, hotel reservations, and convention planning—are looking for employees who speak more than one language. They must be able to provide services for customers from all over the world.

About half of the country's travel agents work in suburban areas and make up a large portion of the travel industry's personnel. They are a key component of the industry even though they have been seriously challenged by the advances in technology that allow travelers to make their own travel plans and to buy their tickets on the Internet.

Agents are more specialized in today's fast-paced world of travel. International agents must provide information on customs regulations, passports, visas, vaccination certificates, and other health-related requirements to remote and exotic places as well as to more standard destinations. Their customers want the latest information on current exchange rates and travel tips of all kinds.

The travel agent's workload varies, depending on the season and the economy. International travelers spent $93 billion in the United States in 2004, according to the TIA. Travel into the United States is influenced by the strength of the dollar and other factors. More tourists visit the United States when the exchange rate is favorable to foreign currencies. Special events such as the Olympics or other international events attract visitors. Sophisticated marketing of travel opportunities also has an effect.

Travelandleisure.com listed the top ten tourism destinations for U.S. residents as Mexico, Canada, United Kingdom, France, Italy, China, Germany, Jamaica, Japan, and the Bahamas. Travel to China increased 72 percent in 2004. Because Americans are not known for their language skills, it stands to reason that an increasing number of multilingual tour guides and travel employees are needed as travelers flock to the popular tourist destinations. Language problems often aggravate ordinary day-to-day problems.

One visitor complained that he was unable to find tasty and nutritious vegetarian meals in those parts of the United States in which he wanted to travel. No one had thought to provide a list of vegetarian eating places where Hindu visitors could eat without violating their religious beliefs.

Being multilingual and having a knowledge of other cultures definitely improves your job prospects. If you work for a travel agency, you can certainly help your North American clients more effectively if you are able to talk to people abroad in the language of their countries.

Working Conditions and Requirements

Travel agents spend most of their time working behind a desk—conferring with clients, punching alternate schedules into a computer in a search for the best rates and connections, making car rental and hotel reservations, and arranging for group travel. During peak travel times, agents typically are under a great deal of pressure, especially if they own their own businesses, and they often work long hours. Pay for beginners is modest. Managers earn better salaries. The travel industry is sensitive to economic recessions, when people tend to put off their travel plans.

Travel agents need good interpersonal skills. You need to be a good salesperson—pleasant, patient, and able to gain the confidence of your clients. The same skills are required for personnel in the airline industry and the hotel and resort fields.

Training

Employers aren't excited about hiring inexperienced travel agents, so how do you get trained? There are several options.

The number of colleges and universities that offer bachelor's and master's degrees in travel and tourism has increased markedly in the last few years. Private vocational schools offer full-time programs lasting from three to twelve weeks. Some schools offer weekend and/or evening courses. Travel and tourism education experts report that most entry-level positions in the travel and tourism industry require little or no formal education. For many, an associate's degree in travel and tourism is more than enough. Many educational institutions offer online programs of study in travel and tourism.

Florida International University School of Hospitality Management and the School of Hotel Administration at Cornell University in the state of New York are noteworthy. The University of Nevada, Las Vegas, is renowned for its William F. Harrah College of Hotel Administration as well as a department of tourism and convention administration. This university is committed to providing cutting-edge educational opportunities in a range of tourism and hospitality fields, including casinos, clubs, conventions and expositions, entertainment, food services, and lodging and resort industries.

Courses in foreign languages, geography, history, and computers use are useful, especially for aspiring travel agents. If you want to start your own travel business and you have experience in the travel industry, courses in accounting and business management also will be helpful.

In addition to courses offered by colleges and vocational schools, training is available from travel associations both in person and online. The American Society of Travel Agents and the Institute of Certified Travel Agents offer courses. Once you become an experienced travel agent, you may want to take an advanced, eighteen-month, part-time course offered by the Institute of Certified Travel Agents. This gives you the title of Certified Travel Counselor. Another recognized mark of achievement is the certificate of proficiency offered by the American Society of Travel Agents to those who pass the three-hour examination.

Whatever course of study you choose, education is an important part of preparing to become part of the travel industry. Two other factors are also key to your success: work experience and travel. On-the-job training is invaluable. You may want to start by taking some courses and then applying for part-time work as an airline reservations clerk or receptionist in the travel industry. With experience and education, you will advance. If you can afford it, travel is another way to make yourself ready for a career in the travel industry. Firsthand experience of vacation spots allows you to better inform clients about what awaits them when they leave for their trips. You can also "travel" by watching videos, accessing websites, and doing other types of research.

The tremendous impact of computer technology on the workplace finds us booking our own travel schedules and buying tickets on the Internet. Many of these websites offer employment opportunities as well. Most have customer service representatives who handle questions from travelers around the globe.

Related Job Opportunities

Many people research and plan their own trips, making their own reservations and travel arrangements and purchasing their own tickets on the Internet. But unless they are "virtual travelers," these people still have to use vehicles—cars, buses, trains, and airplanes—to move from place to place. All kinds of workers are required to help get people to their destinations.

Airport Personnel

Working at an airport can give you an opportunity to practice your language and service skills. The number of jobs in airport security has grown tremendously in the last half-dozen years. Security personnel with foreign language skills are particularly valuable to the airport security industry, but workers from bus drivers and skycaps to food service and security personnel may also be in frequent contact with people who don't speak English and who need assistance or service. If you have people skills and some level of language capability, you can launch a career in tourism and travel by working at an airport.

Airline Personnel

Other opportunities to use foreign language skills come from working directly for the airlines. Pilots and flight attendants assigned to international routes have an obvious chance to speak a language other than English on the job. It takes time and training to be assigned to these positions of responsibility, but the work is well worth considering if you have language skills and an interest in flying. And although language skills are not required for these jobs, knowing another language does give job candidates an edge in a tough market. It also makes assignment to international flights more likely once you have secured a job with the airlines.

Hotel and Motel Employees

Large metropolitan hotel employees who are fluent in many different languages are highly valued. These individuals serve as desk clerks, cashiers, front office personnel, and in other management positions. As tourism increases in the United States, the need for bilingual or multilingual personnel in the hospitality industry—hotels, motels, and restaurants—has expanded from the elite metropolitan establishments to the small hotels, inns, and motels in towns and cities across America and Canada. The way foreign visitors are turning up in places like Hamilton, Ontario; Lawrence, Kansas; and Pensacola, Florida, it is clear that English-only hotel and motel workers may be underprepared to serve incoming guests.

Opportunities and Rewards

The travel industry grew beyond the Department of Labor's expectations for the first seven years of this decade, and there has been a substantial gain in the need for multilingual employees in security, transportation, travel, and tourism.

The *Occupational Outlook Handbook* states that employment of travel agents is expected to decline through 2014. Most openings will occur as experienced agents transfer to other occupations or leave the labor force. Travel agents who specialize and can utilize the Internet to reduce their costs and better compete with other travel suppliers should have the best chance for success. Experience, sales ability, and the size and location of the agency determine the salary of a travel agent. Median annual earnings of travel agents were around $30,000 in May 2007.

Hotel and accommodations work is expected to increase by 17 percent between 2007 and 2014, according to the *Occupational Outlook Handbook*. Recently, business and leisure travelers have resumed travel patterns that were typical before the dramatic decreases seen after September 11, 2001.

Depending on which area of travel and tourism you choose, salaries can range from $22,000 to $40,000. Many positions in the travel and tourism industry work on commission and receive regular bonuses for performance, raising earning potential even higher. Earning a degree in travel and tourism can provide you with an even better salary and a number of perks, depending on the area in which you work. Hotel employees can get free or reduced rates for hotel stays, airline workers get free or discounted tickets, and travel agents get free trips.

Earnings in hotels and other accommodations generally are much lower than the average for all industries. In 2007, average earnings for all nonsupervisory workers in this industry were around $12 an hour. Many workers in this industry earn the federal minimum wage.

Salaries of lodging managers are dependent on their specific duties and responsibilities and upon the size and sales volume of the establishment. Managers may earn bonuses ranging up to 50 percent of their basic salary. In addition, they and their families may be furnished with lodging, meals, parking, laundry, and other services. Some hotels offer profit-sharing plans, tuition reimbursement, and other benefits to their employees.

For More Information

For details on travel careers, contact the following organizations:

Associations

Air Line Pilots Association International
1625 Massachusetts Avenue NW
Washington, DC 20036
www.alpa.org

American Society of Travel Agents (ASTA)
1101 King Street, Suite 200
Alexandria, VA 22314
www.astanet.com

Association of Flight Attendants—CWA
501 Third Street NW
Washington, DC 20001
www.afanet.org

Schools

Algonquin College of Applied Arts and Technology
Tourism and Travel Management
1385 Woodroffe Avenue
Ottawa, ON K2G 1V8
Canada
www.algonquincollege.com

Camosun College
School of Business
Hotel and Restaurant Management
3100 Foul Bay Road
Victoria, BC V8P 5J5
Canada
www.camosun.bc.ca

Cornell University
School of Hotel Administration
Ithaca, NY 14853
www.hotelschool.cornell.edu

Fanshawe College
Tourism and Hospitality
1001 Fanshawe College Boulevard, Room A1015
PO Box 7005
London, ON N5Y 5R6
Canada
www.fanshawec.on.ca/tourism

Florida International University
School of Hospitality and Tourism Management
3000 Northeast 151st Street
North Miami, FL 33181
www.hospitality.fiu.edu

Grant MacEwan Community College
Tourism and Travel Management
PO Box 1796
Edmonton, AB T5J 2P2
Canada
www.macewan.ca

Institute of Certified Travel Agents
The Travel Institute
148 Linden Street, Suite 305
Wellesley, MA 02482
www.thetravelinstitute.com

Malasprina College
Hospitality Management/Tourism Studies
900 Fifth Street
Nanaimo, BC V9R 5S5
Canada
www.mala.ca

Northern Alberta Institute of Technology
Hospitality and Culinary Arts
11762 - 106th Street NW
Edmonton, AB T5G 3H1
Canada
www.nait.ca

Ryerson University
School of Hospitality and Tourism
350 Victoria Street
Toronto, ON M5B 2K3
Canada
www.ryerson.ca

Southern Alberta Institute of Technology
Hotel and Restaurant Management/Travel and Tourism
1301 Sixteenth Avenue NW
Calgary, AB T2M 0L4
Canada
www.sait.ab.ca

University of Nevada Las Vegas
William F. Harrah College of Hotel Administration
4505 Maryland Parkway
Box 456013
Las Vegas, NV 89154
www.unlv.edu/Colleges/Hotel

CHAPTER ELEVEN

Government

ost jobs described so far can be found in one form or
another within the programs of local, state or provincial,
and federal government: social sciences, librarianship, pro-
tection, translation, health care, and more. If you pursue any of
these jobs within these systems, most of what has already been
discussed will apply. The U.S. and Canadian governments maintain job search websites on the Internet. City, state, and provincial
governments also maintain Internet job sites. Privately run websites also give details about jobs in government service. Some of
the most useful are listed at the end of the chapter. You should be
aware that there are unique requirements and responsibilities
involved with working for government.

Requirements

The federal government represents the biggest bureaucracy. You
must be a team worker and be able to deal with the red tape and
intricacies of this huge enterprise. Some people enjoy the connections and interplay and other challenges involved with a complex
system. State or provincial and local government operations mir-
ror, on a smaller scale, those of the federal government. If you are
one of those people who work well within such structures, government jobs can be very satisfying, and they offer increasingly
varied opportunities for multilingual work.

Government jobs have requirements you might not find if you
apply for work elsewhere. Government jobs often demand drug

testing and require you to be fingerprinted. When some level of security clearance is necessary, details of your past may be investigated, and you may be required to take a polygraph test.

Many of the language-related jobs will require travel, which can be a disadvantage or an advantage, depending on your point of view. You may also be required to restrict your involvement with politics to avoid an appearance of conflict of interest.

Opportunities and Rewards

Working for the government at any level is different from working anywhere else. If you are unsure about getting into government work, internships provide a good way to explore the option. Many branches of municipal, state or provincial, and federal government offer both paid and unpaid internships that will give you good firsthand knowledge of multilingual government work. Whether you choose to continue with a government career or decide it is not for you, the experience will prove valuable in improving your language and job skills.

Employment opportunities within government are greater and more far-ranging and varied than many people realize. One of the most difficult parts of getting a job with the government is finding out about openings. One of the best ways to do this is to request job information from the specific department in which you wish to work.

The U.S. Department of State has many jobs that require foreign language proficiency (usually at a 3+ rating on a 5-point rating scale). In the summer of 2007, the U.S. Department of State revised its foreign service officer selection process. It dropped the paper-and-pencil exam and launched a new process that included a somewhat shorter computer-based test and some other innovations. The most common State Department programs that use such ratings are the Foreign Service; Democracy, Human Rights, and Labor; the Bureau of Intelligence and Research; and Population, Refugees, and Migration.

The Agency for International Development is one of several other divisions attached to the State Department that also seek employees with foreign language skills. There are also language-related positions in other government agencies, including the Department of Defense, the National Security Agency, the Central Intelligence Agency, and the Immigration and Naturalization Service.

The pay and advancement for all U.S. civil service jobs is set by the structured guidelines of the federal GS system. Most language-related jobs will fall in the GS-5 to GS-11 range. The U.S. Office of Personnel Management maintains a website where you can find pay scales for civil service jobs and other government employment: www.opm.gov/feddata/html/paystructure.

Employees in "excepted" service jobs receive similar pay but are not subject to the same exam and testing procedures, nor are they affected by other GS guidelines such as extra points for veteran status. Excepted jobs are sometimes offered on limited contracts and sometimes last only for a finite contract period. Benefits such as retirement, saving plans, insurance, and leave are very good for civil service jobs, and often these are extended to excepted service employees. You can find specific salaries for specific jobs in the United States and other countries at www.payscale.com. States, provinces, and municipalities have their own civil service systems.

Language and Cultural Proficiency

Language proficiency to qualify for a job is based heavily on tests. Most U.S. departments rely on the Foreign Service Institute or Inter-Agency Language Round Table proficiency ratings, which rate prospective employees from zero to five, according to the results of the testing. (The Canadian foreign service has a similar employment testing program. For information, visit the website at www.international.gc.ca/department/service/menu-en.asp.) Written, structured testing is not always the most accurate way of judging language and communication skills, however. And, if your on-the-job performance does not match the level estimated by the test, you will be let go.

The particular languages most in demand depend on current political circumstances. At this writing, the languages most in demand are Arabic (and dialects), Chinese (and dialects), Russian, Korean, Japanese, Farsi, and Polish.

In addition to language skills, prospective government employees should have an interest in other cultures and in living abroad. They should be able to adapt quickly to the country where they are assigned. Sometimes this means adjustments in lifestyle. For example, Anthony, an employee of the Agency for International Development, was stationed in Afghanistan. He reports that one of the strains of living in Muslim countries is the social restriction on public displays of affection, even with a spouse. Hand holding and good-bye kisses are to be avoided. Even in the privacy of your home, you must exercise discretion because the servants may be offended and report the offensive behavior to their friends and associates. However, Anthony adjusted, and he enjoyed many fruitful years living in various Muslim countries.

Law Enforcement, Corrections, and Firefighting

In communities all over the country, people work for government agencies in law enforcement, corrections, and firefighting, providing essential public services to citizens and immigrants alike. This often requires foreign language skills in sometimes difficult situations.

Members of the U.S. and Canadian police, security officers and related personnel, corrections officers, and firefighters render vital services to their nations. Persons in these occupations are generally highly respected. However, these jobs can be dangerous and stressful for both those working in the field and for their families. You need to consider that this work would bring you into contact with some unpleasant aspects of society, at home and sometimes abroad. It takes toughness to face this sort of work day after day. At the same time, direct service to your country and community offers many rewards, and many find great satisfaction in these jobs.

Requirements and Training

A high school diploma or the equivalent is required for jobs within these fields. There are also citizenship requirements. Training beyond high school is also required, and the length and type of training depends on the job you are seeking. Many universities and community colleges offer one- and two-year programs in security, law enforcement, and related fields. Police, fire, and corrections departments offer training academies. Workers must have good written and verbal communication skills. Gathering data, interviewing witnesses, keeping records, taking notes, and writing clear and concise reports are important parts of all of these occupations.

The need for bilingual and multilingual skills in these occupations is increasing all over the nation. More and more people, particularly in large cities but even smaller communities, do not speak English as their primary language, and some do not speak English at all. For law enforcement personnel, being able to communicate with these people in their primary languages has many advantages. And possessing the language skills necessary to do so will make you very valuable and improve your performance and safety on the job. Your language skills need to be such that people speaking with you will be confident that they are being understood, and you must be sure you are understood by them as well. Schoolbook perfection is not required; it's knowing the language of the street and the expressions of the specific subcultures with which you will be dealing that is important.

Employers are especially seeking people who are part of the communities that they will serve. In times of stress and danger, language can be the difference between life and death, and the benefits are enhanced when the officer or firefighter not only speaks the language but is identifiable as a member of the community group. Current literature and projections for the future specifically mention a great need for Arabic, Latino, and Chinese language proficiencies and backgrounds in these occupations.

Police Enforcement

Police officers are increasingly required to exhibit social and cultural sensitivity. If you have an interest in law enforcement at the local, state or provincial, or national level, your efforts will be enhanced by language and cultural skills. Even in small communities in rural settings, police and sheriff's department personnel are being hired because of their skills in a second language. At the state level, the highway patrol and state investigative agencies are seeking officers and detectives with language skills. The FBI and other federal government law enforcement organizations all have policies that call for increased numbers of second language qualified personnel.

Serious disturbances have erupted when English-speaking police officers have confronted members of ethnic minorities for behavior that, within their culture, was acceptable. In one instance in Washington, D.C., a police arrest brought about a riot that resulted in a great deal of property damage and a curfew imposed on the area. Significantly, of the five thousand or so police officers in the District of Columbia where the riot occurred, fewer than a hundred spoke Spanish at the time, and few of those were stationed in the Spanish-speaking parts of the city. Things have changed significantly in D.C. and other places. Hiring officers with second language skills can be a very cost-effective way to improve the relationship between the police and the community in tense times.

The Royal Canadian Mounted Police (RCMP), the Canadian national police service, is an agency of the Ministry of Public Safety and Emergency Preparedness Canada. The RCMP maintains a national job registry online at www.rcmp-grc.ca. Since

Canada is by law bilingual in French and English, the RCMP and other law enforcement agencies offer opportunities for multilingual job seekers.

Corrections

People who work in protective services and correctional centers need a strong sense of social justice and responsibility. Corrections officers work with people who have broken the law or have had some other brush with the legal system. In these situations, there is a great need for people who can explain the laws and the legal system to people whose primary language is not English and who may not understand their rights and responsibilities. As social diversity continues to increase, more people with language skills are needed in law enforcement and corrections positions.

Security

The war on terrorism has increased the need for security workers of all kinds. People who work in airport security, for example, deal with thousands of people a day. Many of them need help in complying with security regulations. If they are non-English speakers, they appreciate and need those people who have language and cross-cultural skills.

According to the website www.jobssearchtech.about.com, hiring for employment in airport security jobs was done exclusively by the Transportation Security Administration (TSA) after the September 11 terrorist attacks. Then, in November 2004, the TSA started accepting applications from private screening companies under its Screening Partnership Program.

Firefighters

Like law enforcement personnel, firefighters are found in all communities and are responsible for protecting all segments of the community. In large cities where there are large foreign language communities concentrated in certain areas, it may be a matter of life or death for firefighters to be able to understand victims of fires or explosions. In this job, a lack of communication can be life threatening.

Opportunities and Rewards

Job growth from the rising demand for services is expected to increase employment in state and local governments by 11 percent through 2014. Earnings vary by occupation, size of the state or locality, and region of the country.

As in most industries, professionals and managers earn more than other workers. Hourly wages ranged in 2007 from around $14 an hour for secretaries and clerks to around $25 an hour for law enforcement officers.

For More Information

For detailed information on jobs with the federal government, visit the official U.S. government job search website at www .usajobs.opm.gov. Individual federal departments and agencies maintain websites that contain valuable information. The U.S. Department of State, for example, can be contacted by logging on to www.state.gov.

At the Bureau of Labor Statistics website (www.bls.gov), you'll find information about wages, earnings and benefits, production statistics, safety and health data, international labor figures, and demographic data.

Each state maintains a website that lists employment possibilities. These sites can usually be accessed by typing www.(name of state).gov (for example, the Idaho website address would be www.idaho.gov).

The Canadian government's employment programs can be found at the Public Service Commission of Canada's bilingual website, www.jobs-emplois.gc.ca.

Additional Canadian resources may be found at:

Indian and Northern Affairs Canada
www.ainc-inac.gc.ca

Public Service Commission of Canada
www.psc-cfp.gc.ca
  Manages the hiring process for the federal civil service in Canada

Service Canada
Federal Public Sector Youth Internship Program
www.servicecanada.gc.ca/en/sc/youth/youthinternship.shtml

CHAPTER TWELVE

Language-Intensive Jobs: Translating, Interpreting, Teaching

By the time Turkish writer Orhan Pamuk found an English translator for his second novel, *Snow*, he was getting desperate, wrote Joy Stocke in a *Writer's Digest* article. Pamuk had worked with, and lost, three translators. He turned to an old friend, Maureen Freely, to translate *Snow*. The arrangement worked out for them both when the book became a bestseller. Pamuk said that even though he speaks fluent English, it was crucial to have a good translator. "*Snow* would never have found success in America without Maureen," said Pamuk.

Translating, interpreting, and teaching are jobs people tend to think of first when seeking ways to use their foreign language skills. These occupations all require exceptional written and oral fluency in the target language.

Translating and Interpreting

Translators and interpreters transfer information from one language to another. Translators work with written information, and interpreters with spoken information. Both try to achieve minimum distortion of meaning in the process. An article in *Writer's*

Digest describes translating works of fiction as the art of remaining true to the writers' visions. Not only should the message of the translation or interpretation be the same as the original, but the style and emotional content of the statement should be comparable to the original. A good translator or interpreter does not impose his or her own style, interpretation, or opinion onto the translation.

Just because a person is bilingual does not mean that he or she will be a good translator or, especially, a good interpreter. Some people have a special gift for this work and even they must train and practice to be effective.

There are more than ten thousand translators and interpreters working in the United States, many working only part-time. The market tendency seems to favor interpreters over translators. Since the Canadian government processes its official documents in English and French, there are many more translators and interpreters in Canada per capita than in the United States.

Job Requirements

Both translators and interpreters require the highest level of second-language skills. Translators almost always translate from the second language into their native language, but this is not always the case with interpreters. Both of these occupations require extensive knowledge of the native language as well as the second language and require, as well, a sound understanding of the culture or cultures associated with the target language.

Translators must be meticulous students of language patterns, grammar, and idiomatic meaning. Persons interested in interpretation should be good with people, be good listeners, and have clear speech. Nuance and accent can be very important in oral communication. Employers of interpreters are usually high government or business officials. Therefore, an understanding of protocol, customs, and etiquette is essential for interpreters who wish to efficiently and unobtrusively facilitate conversation between the parties they are interpreting for.

Those interested in careers in this area need more than fluency in a second language; knowledge in a variety of subjects is also helpful. Translators and interpreters alike should read widely in the language they will be translating. Newspapers, magazines, catalogs, and general materials of all sorts are helpful. Travel in countries where the language is spoken is invaluable, especially for the interpreter. Most interpreters have spoken several languages all of their lives. United Nations interpreters need native or near-native fluency in at least three of the six official languages of the United Nations: Arabic, Chinese, English, French, Russian, and Spanish. These positions are very competitive.

The translator may hone his or her skills through courses in journalism and technical writing. Familiarity with the jargon of many fields will greatly enhance the value of a translator or interpreter. Some universities offer special translator/interpreter training programs. Russian, German, Japanese, French, and Spanish are the languages most in demand, but there is a growing need for interpreters and translators in Portuguese, Chinese, and Arabic. A couple of broad areas of knowledge (math, science, business), in addition to extensive language skills, will enable the interpreter or translator to have the greatest number of career options.

Research skills are important for interpreters and translators. The Internet has made research easier and more rapid, but researchers must be careful to access websites that carry valid and authentic information.

Computer translation programs have proliferated in recent years, and there are automated Internet translation services. These translation innovations have not replaced the need for professionally trained translators and interpreters. If have a variety of interests, possess excellent primary and secondary language skills, have a good memory, and like writing or meeting new people, this might be the career for you.

Employers

The federal government is the largest single employer of transla-
tors and interpreters. The federal agencies include the State
Department, Federal Bureau of Investigation, National Security
Agency, Central Intelligence Agency, Agency for International
Development, Library of Congress, U.S. District Courts, and the
U.S. Information Agency.

The need for interpreters and translators, particularly in the
court systems at all levels, has increased greatly in the past ten
years. Interpreters often work in the court systems on a freelance
basis. They interpret documents and the depositions of witnesses
who do not speak English and provide interpretation for judges,
attorneys, and other officers of the court.

State and municipal governments also require interpreters and
translators. Canada's bilingual status encourages the development
of language skills and fosters job development on many fronts.
One of the best places to find out about bilingual and multilingual
translation and interpretation opportunities is through the Canadian Translators, Terminologists, and Interpreters Council. Its
bilingual website is www.cttic.org. The Canadian foreign service,
the Royal Canadian Mounted Police, Canadian government security organizations, the Library of Parliament, the Canadian court
system, and agencies similar to those in the United States hire
translators, terminologists, and interpreters.

Other employers include the United Nations, international
agencies such as the International Development Bank, the
Telecommunications Satellite Organization, the Organization of
American States, the Pan-American Health Organization, and
some private industries. Frequently, translators are self-employed
people who are contracted by companies to translate a personnel
manual or a piece of business correspondence. Large international
companies such as IBM have full-time translators on staff.
Guadalupe, an English-Spanish-Portuguese translator working
for an international electronics firm, specializes in technical documents and has a team of translators working for her. Translators

and interpreters will have more job opportunities if they know several languages.

Many American service organizations and businesses employ workers who take on valuable translation and interpretation assignments from time to time even though their primary jobs are not language related. These employers consider a second language a very valuable secondary skill.

Foreign Language Teaching

We are all familiar with foreign language teaching; many of us have enrolled in foreign language classes. Perhaps you have been inspired to use your second language by a grade school, high school, or college foreign language teacher. In the current job market, these teaching jobs can be competitive, but the demand is rising. Jobs at the primary or secondary school level require a bachelor's degree—often a master's degree—plus teacher certification, which involves an additional one or two years of education courses.

At least 20 percent of elementary schools and 90 percent of secondary schools offer foreign language instruction. Most of these jobs are for Spanish, French, German, and Latin, in descending order of popularity. Career opportunities on the college level are usually for adjunct, rather than full-time, instructors. Many undergraduate college students are taught by graduate teaching assistants, especially at larger universities.

Bilingual Education Programs

Currently, it is easier to find jobs in bilingual education than it is in foreign language teaching. Bilingual programs are for students whose grasp of the English language is so limited that they can be better educated having subject matter taught in their native language. Bilingual teachers, most of whom are employed on the primary school level, may teach science, math, social studies, or language arts—in the students' native language.

Employers (school superintendents and principals) look for people who are fluent in the requisite language. This is most commonly Spanish in the United States, but it could be any one of a number of other languages. At Fort Lauderdale High School in Florida, students spoke more than fifty different languages. Prospective bilingual teachers need to have a college degree (or two) and be interested in taking the education courses required for state certification if they do not already possess it. If you are interested in teaching in a bilingual program, and there is a community in your area whose language and culture you know, call the local school superintendent to find out the prospects. See Chapter 3 for more information about a related field, teaching English as a second language.

Anthropology

Anthropology teachers often find fluency in a second language to be especially useful. Anthropologists study the origins, cultures, traditions, beliefs, politics, and social relationships of the world's people. They often live abroad for extended periods, and they may hold teaching positions in universities or colleges. A Ph.D. is generally required for teaching at the university level.

Political Science

Political science is another area of teaching in which language fluency is helpful. Political scientists study government at all levels, from the smallest native village to the international community of nations. Foreign language skills are important not only to those who are concerned with international relations and foreign political systems, but also to those interested in the dynamics of local politics. Cross-cultural and linguistic interaction plays an important part in local elections, community development plans, and community solidarity efforts. If you have special interest in politics, the development of your language and cultural skills can help move your career plans forward.

Opportunities and Rewards

According to the *Occupational Outlook Handbook*, employment of interpreters and translators is projected to increase faster than the average for all occupations through 2014. This increase reflects strong growth in the industries employing interpreters and translators. Higher demand for interpreters and translators results directly from broadening international activities and the increase in the number of foreign language speakers in the United States.

Salaries of interpreters and translators vary widely. Earnings depend on the language, subject matter, skill, experience, education, certification, and type of employer. Salaried interpreters and translators had median hourly earnings of around $17 in 2007.

Freelance translators are generally paid by the number of words (or pages), either in the original or the translation. Rates of compensation vary depending on the difficulty of the target languages and the nature of the documents. A good freelance translator can earn a decent living and enjoy the benefit of a flexible work schedule. Freelance interpreters who are certified as U.S. District or Circuit Court interpreters currently earn more than $150 for a half day or more than $300 for a full day.

Salaries for teachers vary by the size and education level of the institution, region of the country, and years of experience. Median annual earnings range from $45,000 for elementary through high school teachers to approximately $68,000 for college and university faculty.

For More Information

The following professional associations offer information about language-intensive careers in translating, interpreting, and teaching. Often the websites provide information about training and education as well as employment opportunities.

American Council on the Teaching of Foreign Languages
    (ACTFL)
700 South Washington Street, Suite 210
Alexandria, VA 22314
www.actfl.org

American Association of Language Specialists
PO Box 39339
Washington, DC 20016
www.taals.net

American Literary Translators Association
Box 830688, Mail Station JO51
University of Texas at Dallas
Richardson, TX 75083
www.literarytranslators.org

American Translators Association (ATA)
225 Reinekers Lane, Suite 590
Alexandria, VA 22314
www.atanet.org

Canadian Translators, Terminologists and Interpreters Council
    (CTTIC)
1 Nicholas Street, Suite 1202
Ottawa, ON K1N 7B7
Canada
www.cttic.org

National Clearinghouse for English Language Acquisition &
    Language Instruction Educational Programs
2121 K Street NW, Suite 260
Washington, DC 20037
www.ncela.gwu.edu

National Association for Bilingual Education (NABE)
1030 Fifteenth Street NW
Washington, DC 20005
www.nabe.org

Society of Federal Linguists (SFL)
PO Box 7765
Washington, DC 20044
www.federal-linguists.org

Consulting

···

onsultants are independent specialists who help clients. "The essence of management consulting is to help a client obtain information and advice which leads to a real and lasting solution of a problem," according to "Careers in Consulting," an online article at www.careers-in-business.com. The article continues: "Consultants think, analyze, brainstorm, cajole and challenge good organizations to become even better by adopting new ideas. Great consultants are able to step into ambiguous, sometimes hostile situations and sense what changes need to be made. Great consultants are driven by ideas and a strong desire to have a positive impact on clients."

If you have some particular expertise that is in demand, you may want to explore employment as a national or international consultant. In most cases, businesses look for consultants with a graduate degree and significant experience related to their specialization. Clients also want consultants who speak the language of the country that needs their expertise.

What kinds of expertise are in demand? Information technology (IT) specialists will be in high demand in the United States, Canada, and internationally for the rest of this decade and beyond, according to employment experts. But there are many more areas of expertise in demand. Experienced consultants are needed in rural health care, including nutrition and family planning; rural educational development; adult literacy; agriculture; and civil engineering.

Jerry was in Iraq during his last three years as a U.S. Marine officer. He retired after more than twenty-five years in the military and within months was back in Iraq, working as a highly paid consultant for a business firm. Jerry knew people in Iraq. He knew the culture and he knew the problems the firm was facing as it fulfilled its contracts. Jerry made a lot more money for a year-long assignment as a consultant in Iraq than he had made as a military officer doing some of the same things in some of the same places.

Requirements

Usually about ten years of experience is needed to be competitive as a consultant. Previous work in the host country is highly desirable, although not normally expected. Familiarity with, and an understanding of, the host country's culture, infrastructure (both physical and political), and other pertinent facts considerably enhance your prospects.

To be competitive for most of these opportunities, you must not only be able to do the job, you must be able to convince a stranger reading your curriculum vitae (a long, more academic type of resume) that your education and training equip you to do the job. In other words, you have to inspire confidence on paper. A master's degree is generally the lowest level of academic preparation sought; a doctorate is better. Either of these academic degrees, added to several years of experience in or familiarity with the area, region, or country, would set off green lights for the person reviewing your resume.

For much of Africa, English and French are all that most agencies can realistically require. Fluency in particular African languages, of which there are hundreds, would be an asset for community development work where those languages are spoken.

Spanish is the language requirement for much of Latin America, although it's Portuguese for Brazil. Occasionally, and depending on how deeply into the interior of the country you may need to go, a native South American language may be useful.

Consultants fluent in Asian languages have a distinct advantage in landing assignments in that area.

Opportunities and Rewards

A lot of companies hire international consultants, according to an international job search website (www.careerframes.com). For example, Accenture, formerly Andersen Consulting, had more than seventy thousand professionals working in forty-six countries in 2007. Arthur D. Little did technology and environmental consulting from offices worldwide. Hewitt Associates operated seventy-nine offices in thirty-seven countries, where it specialized in human resource consulting. A number of international companies are listed, with their websites, in Appendix B.

From this list, you can identify companies that from time to time may be in need of someone with your special skills. To learn more about other companies on the list, research their websites or look them up in the reference section of your local library. Some of these companies may not be doing as much international business now as they were a few years ago, and others might have changed focus.

Many international companies keep a bank of resumes on hand, unlike most domestic companies, and they often welcome receiving yours. But having your resume on hand does not mean they will actively pursue you. You will have to follow up if an interview is arranged. Don't assume you are in their line of sight. Check back periodically and hammer home your availability.

A typical short-term assignment overseas as a consultant may involve working closely with several people from the funding agency and the national host on a four- to six-week project. The contracts often stipulate a long list of tasks that must be completed. The hours are long; the real workweek is often seven days. Your task may be to figure out how to get the project's objectives accomplished without rubbing people the wrong way. Sometimes a fifty- to one-hundred-page report must be written for and approved by the funding source.

Government agencies or multinational corporations that hire consultants usually have preset compensation scales, but they occasionally defer to your specified level of compensation if you are employed full-time and take an assignment on a special basis. When that is the case, some agencies may calculate your daily wage by dividing your annual income by 260 workdays in a year. There are rarely any fringe benefits other than a per diem, which may differ according to living costs in the host country.

Landing a Consulting Contract

The majority of consulting contracts are with large companies. Funding agencies find their consultants by looking through their banks of resumes or curriculum vitae and by calling contacts who suggest names to them. You must sell yourself to a company, which then submits your curriculum vita to the funding agency, usually along with the curriculum vitae of two or three other qualified candidates. The funding agency will select the consultant it wants. Some longer-term contracts also may be made for periods of one to five years. The compensation package generally is good, and there are generous housing allowances.

Starting Your Own Consulting Business

Unless you are well known or well connected, starting your own business is a hard route to go. Most agencies, in spite of professed interest in small companies, want to contract with large companies or universities.

For a list of employers involved with international consulting, see Appendix B.

CHAPTER FOURTEEN

Developing a Job-Search Strategy

job search is a marketing campaign, writes employment expert Dawn Rosenberg McKay in her online newsletter, "Your Guide to Career Planning" (www.careerplanning .about.com). According to McKay, as a job or career seeker, you should realize that you are the "product" that is being marketed. With that in mind, you can identify the types of employers who are looking for someone with your qualifications.

Your job and career search capabilities have been multiplied manyfold by technology. Vast electronic resources are available on the Internet. However, the *Wall Street Journal* reported that job searches conducted solely online rarely produce jobs. So be prudent. Diversify your job search and your approaches to a career path.

Today's career specialists generally agree on job-search strategies. Here are seven simple steps.

1. Look within yourself.
2. Research your career field.
3. Get out a resume.
4. Network to refine your job search.
5. Obtain informational (not job) interviews.
6. Interview for jobs you want.
7. Negotiate a job package that suits you.

Looking Within

Before you start your job search, you should think about your long-term career aspirations, according to Stephanie Lowell, who wrote a career guide for Harvard Business School. You should write down the experiences you've had and the skills you've developed. What organizational characteristics do you like and dislike (such as size and location)? What do you care about? What would you enjoy enough to do every day, perhaps for years to come?

Researching Your Career Field

There are hundreds of Internet websites where you can gauge your skills, post your resume, and browse job listings. Let's say that you're interested in international organizations. There are many. Here are five basic kinds:

1. **Public multinational** (United Nations, World Bank, International Monetary Fund, Organization of American States, European Common Market, North Atlantic Treaty Organization, Organization for Economic Cooperation and Development)
2. **Government** (Department of State, Department of Defense, U.S. military forces, Agency for International Development, Department of Agriculture, Central Intelligence Agency, Federal Bureau of Investigation, National Security Agency, Peace Corps, AmeriCorps*VISTA in the United States; Foreign Service, Royal Canadian Mounted Police, Agriculture and Agri-Food of Canada, Department of National Defense and Canadian Forces, Canadian Security Intelligence Service, Volunteer Service Overseas in Canada)
3. **Business** (banks, Internet companies, manufacturing companies, consulting firms)

4. **Educational** (American Field Service, Council on International Educational Exchange, Institute on International Education, foundations, universities)
5. **Private voluntary** (Partners of the Americas, CARE, Save the Children, Foster Parents Plan, Salvation Army, Habitat for Humanity, Red Cross, YMCA/YWCA).

It's important to understand the kind of employee each type of organization seeks. For example, unless you have years of relevant experience and prestigious university degrees, public multinationals are difficult to break into. Some government agencies are extremely competitive also. For example, only one in ninety-three applicants to the State Department gets a job there. The Peace Corps, contrary to the popular image, accepts people of all ages—if they have skills that are needed in developing nations. Businesses generally want you to spend a year or so in the United States or Canada, learning what the company is all about, before sending you trekking to an overseas post. Educational and private voluntary organizations often require special contacts to smooth the way to an international job.

Developing a Resume

The purpose of a resume is not to get a job; it is to get an interview that may lead to a job. When you go to the interview, you want to take a copy of your resume with you. Going to an interview without a resume in your pocket is a big mistake.

There are scores of online programs to help you create a resume. First, it is crucial to know your own qualifications. Do you, for example, have the background and skills that are valued by the people who will hire you in an international job? If so, you will want to highlight these skills in your resume.

Next, it's important to have a career objective. Many resumes state a career objective at the beginning. Often the best place for a specific objective is in a cover letter rather than in the resume. (You don't want to limit your options, do you?) Still, it is a good idea to include a general career objective on your resume that is specific enough to show that you have a definite goal. Then you can state a more specific objective in each cover letter.

There are two general formats for resumes: chronological and functional. A chronological sequence is probably best for most recent graduates or those who have followed a steady career progression in the same or related fields. If you have been out of the workforce for some time, if your career has had long interruptions, or if you are making a drastic change in careers, then the functional format may be best for you. In this format you focus on achievements and skills. If you are in doubt of which format to use, use the chronological format. It is more conservative, and the people who do the hiring tend to be conservative themselves.

Once you have reviewed your qualifications, formulated an objective, and selected a resume format, it's time to focus on language. Clear, concise, and active are the key concepts here. You want to sound professional, intelligent, and warm. It is easy to fall into boring prose and irritating jargon. Don't do it. It will be worth your while to pick up a manual or go online to get ideas for preparing your resume. (See the bibliography at the end of this chapter.) There are a number of helpful software programs to enable you to turn out a professional-looking resume on a personal computer. Whatever you do, don't misspell any words, and don't lie about your work or educational background.

While you must be honest, you do want to play up your strengths. Describe what skills and accomplishments you had in your jobs (if they are relevant to the kind of job you are seeking). North American executives love hard numbers. Quantify anything that you can: you were one of two secretaries in a department of eight professional epidemiologists, handling an average of eighty-six pieces of correspondence and 120 requests for information weekly over a computer network linking 843 health centers specializing in fourteen contagious diseases. You get the point.

And it is equally important to disguise your weaknesses. Some things that are generally considered weaknesses include a short time in a job and being between jobs for more than a few months at a time. These can be finessed by omitting some jobs you were in for only a short time and by rounding off dates to just the year.

If you studied or traveled between jobs, be sure to make that clear. If you did volunteer work, by all means list it. Unpaid experience should be described in the same ways that you describe paid job experience. And don't forget to quantify.

You will want to include a section on education in your resume. If you are straight out of school or if you have a doctorate, list the education section first. If not, list it after the section on professional experience. If you have a college degree, omit reference to your high school experience (unless you were the valedictorian). List your college grade point average only if it was quite high. Don't list extracurricular activities unless they have a direct bearing on the job you are trying to get. If you attended college for less than one year, then list the relevant courses.

Be very selective about the "optional" information you include on your resume. By all means include any special skills (computer skills, foreign languages) or professional awards. But think twice before you list anything that will turn off a conservative employer. Avoid controversy if you can. If your volunteer experience is with political or social groups that may be seen as controversial, you might want to generalize. You could mention that you were involved in civic affairs and community-development projects without naming names. Better still, exclude these items unless they are directly relevant to the job you are seeking. If they are relevant, give specific details.

Finally, you want to make your resume easy to read. Keep it brief—one or two pages if you possibly can. Prospective employers tend to read only one page. Use white or beige paper (use twenty- or twenty-four-pound paper) and black ink. Provide white space (margins), and use a standard typeface (not script or Old English).

If you conduct your job search online, be sure that you include key words—industry terms, company names, years of experience, degrees—in your resume Your electronic resume could also include links to your personal website if you have one, as well as key industry terms, company names, years of experience, and education.

Websites, Blogs, and Cover Letters

If you have the expertise, the inclination, and enough material to maintain a website, that is a good way to showcase your abilities and interests. Writing a career-oriented blog is a way to keep in touch with people, events, and activities in your field. Here's a word of caution: if you neglect your website, it will be worse than not having one at all.

When applying by mail, always send a one-page, single-spaced cover letter with your resume. When applying online, follow the protocol indicated on the website. In any case, you should state your case—explain what job you want and why.

Make the information look great. It should be neat and concise, with no spelling or grammar errors. Use plain paper; no letterheads unless you own the company. Address the letter to a specific person, not to a job title, when you can. If you don't know the person's name and title, call the company's switchboard and ask the receptionist, or go online and try to find out.

Like the resume, the cover letter should be brief, usually three paragraphs. In the first paragraph, catch the reader's attention: "Your advertisement in the *Wall Street Journal* caught my eye." Mention your objective in the first paragraph as well. In the second paragraph, sell your accomplishments. Quantify where you can. In the final paragraph, be specific about your plans to contact the organization after the reader receives your letter. Don't wait to receive a reply! Initiative is appreciated and conveys enthusiasm.

Networking

Some of your best career contacts may be right under your nose. Your uncle, your doctor, and the person who cuts your hair all have one thing in common: they are part of your network, and they may be able to introduce you to people they know who work in the career field you're interested in. Networking is an essential ingredient of any career-building strategy. Identify a dozen of your family, neighborhood professionals, and personal contacts you know best. Ask them to give you the names of three people they know who work in the particular field you are interested in. Ask them how you should introduce yourself. Oftentimes your friend or colleague will offer to pave the way by calling or writing a letter of introduction.

Send each of your new contacts a package containing a personalized cover letter describing your career goals and a list of the companies you want to work for. Follow up with a telephone call. It's a good idea to practice your phone technique in advance. You may want to write out a short script that is concise and says exactly what you want to get across. Ask your contact if he or she knows anyone in any of the fields in which you are looking for a job.

Ask the local reference librarian for leads. And, of course, go online. Visit professional and occupational websites and log on to blogs that are aimed at people with the same interest that you have.

Lois wanted a job in the Washington, D.C., area that would involve working with Asian refugees. She didn't know what kind of job her background would qualify her for, much less where to apply for a job. One of her professors gave Lois the name of a Mr. Chin, a prominent person in the field of intercultural communication who worked in the Washington area. Lois called, used her professor's name, and asked for an interview. The professor was known to Mr. Chin, and he readily agreed to a meeting. During the meeting, Mr. Chin went out of his way to suggest several general categories of jobs for which Lois would be qualified. Then he suggested several agencies she might want to contact. Lois went to the one that looked most interesting, told the director that Mr. Chin had suggested she contact them, and a week later Lois was working for the agency.

Identifying Contacts

Once you evaluate in what general field you want to get a job, ask yourself several questions. Where do people in this field get together? How am I going to meet them? Who are the wheeler-dealers in the field? The answers are simple. The logical place where practitioners in a field gather is at their annual conferences or trade shows or at their websites and blogs. Type the keywords into an Internet search engine or go to the library and read the trade journals. Often there are a number of conferences. Pick one that's near where you live and attend it.

Studying websites and blogs and skimming trade journals comes in handy now, when you want to meet people. Jot down the names of some of the people who have websites or have published blogs or printed articles you enjoyed and look for them on the conference program. Attend the presentation and talk to them afterward ("I really enjoyed your article on community development projects in Papua New Guinea. . . ."). Ask them to suggest leads for you to follow ("Where should I begin to look for a job that will lead to an overseas posting in community development?").

Interviews

Once you have obtained the names of prospective companies and organizations, do your homework. Learn about your target organization's products or services, its competition, and its organizational structure. Again, the Internet will be a great boon to you here. Virtually every company or organization has a website. You may find the names of individuals strategically placed in the organization in which you are interested. Next, call that person using the most appropriate name in your network and say something like, "Ms. Wilson, Dr. Brown suggested I contact you. He said you might be able to help me in the field." Ask for an informational interview.

There are three phases to any interview: preparation, the interview, and follow-up.

Preparation

Learn something about the person you are going to interview and something about his or her organization. Jot down a few questions to ask ("What job do you think someone of my background might qualify for?" "What's the current job market in this area?" "Can you suggest some people I could talk to about the field?")

Interview

Listen carefully, be polite, and be at ease. Focus on the interview. Watch for nonverbal cues. Don't appear bored or distracted. Leave when you get a signal that the contact person wants to get back to his or her work.

Follow-Up

Send a thank-you note. Online messages are acceptable, but a nicely written, mailed thank-you card will be appreciated. Your contact person didn't have to take time out of his or her schedule to see you. If you get a job as a result of another contact the person gave you, thank the person for that, too.

There are dozens of excellent online websites that give specific job interview instructions. Many books and chapters in books give successful techniques for job interviews. (Those techniques are similar to those used in informational interviews.) Some good sources are listed below. Read one or two of them, and then go for it! There are many international jobs out there for foreign language aficionados.

For More Information

Websites
Following are some of the resources on the Internet:

Monster.com
www.monster.com
A comprehensive job search website

CareerBuilder.com
www.careerbuilder.com
A comprehensive job search website

CareerInfoNet
www.acinet.org
A resource for making informed career decisions

Flipdog
www.flipdog.com
Jobs by city, state, or category

Jobs.com
www.jobs.com
Local and international jobs by location

MultilingualVacancies.com
www.multilingualvacancies.com
European multilingual job website

Creative Job Search (CJS) Online Guide
www.deed.state.mn.us/cjs
*A good online resource for job search strategies and resume
development developed by the Minnesota Department of
Employment and Economic Development*

CampusAccess.com
www.campusaccess.com
A searchable online job guide with many other job-related resources

Books
These books provide detailed information on job searches.

International Job Finder: Where the Jobs Are Worldwide by Daniel
Lauber and Kraig Rice, 2002.
*Nonprofits Job Finder: Where the Jobs Are in Charities and
Nonprofits*, 5th ed., by Daniel Lauber and Jennifer Atkin, 2006.
*The Book of U.S. Government Jobs: Where They Are, What's
Available & How to Get One*, 9th ed., by Dennis V. Damp,
2005.

State and Provincial Offices of Volunteerism

M ost states and provinces have a department, commission, or office dedicated to encouraging volunteers to participate in service to their communities. For information about volunteer opportunities in your area, contact the office nearest you. The U.S. government also has a general website that allows you to search for volunteer opportunities by state: www.volunteer.gov.

Alabama

Governor's Office of Faith Based and Community Initiatives
100 North Union Street, Suite 134
Montgomery, AL 36104
www.goncs.state.al.us

Alaska

Alaska State Community Service Commission
550 West Seventh Street
Anchorage, AK 99501
www.commerce.state.ak.us/ascsc/home.htm

Arizona

Governor's Commission on Service & Volunteerism
1700 West Washington Street, Suite 101
Phoenix, AZ 85007
www.volunteerarizona.org

Arkansas

Arkansas Department of Health & Human Services
Donaghey Plaza South
PO Box 1437, Slot S201
Little Rock, AR 72203
www.arkansas.gov/dhhs/homepage.html

British Columbia

Volunteer BC
302 – 207 W Hastings Street
Vancouver, BC V6B 1H7
Canada
www.volunteerbc.bc.ca

California

California Volunteers
Office of the Governor
1110 K Street, Suite 210
Sacramento, CA 95814
www.californiavolunteers.org/index.asp

Colorado

Governor's Commission on Community Service
1600 Broadway, Suite 1030
Denver, CO 80202
www.colorado.gov/gccs

Connecticut

Connecticut Commission on National and Community
  Service
Department of Higher Education
61 Woodland Street
Hartford, CT 06105
www.ctdhe.org/default.htm

Delaware

Division of State Service Centers
Charles Debnam Building
1901 North DuPont Highway
New Castle, DE 19720
www.workworld.org

District of Columbia

Department of Employment Services
609 H Street NE
Washington, DC 20002
www.does.dc.gov

Florida

The Governor's Commission on Volunteerism and
Community Service, Volunteer Florida
The Elliot Building
401 South Monroe Street
Tallahassee, FL 32301
www.fccs.org

Georgia

Georgia Department of Community Affairs
60 Executive Park South NE
Atlanta, GA 30329
www.dca.state.ga.us

Hawaii

State Volunteer Services
Office of the Governor
State Capitol, Room 415
Honolulu, HI 96801
www.hawaii.gov

Idaho

Serve Idaho
Governor's Commission on Service and Volunteerism
1299 North Orchard, Suite 110
PO Box 83720
Boise, ID 83706
www.serveidaho.org

Illinois

Governor's Hometown Awards Program
Department of Commerce and Economic Opportunity
620 East Adams Street
Springfield, IL 62701
www.commerce.state.il.us

Indiana

Office of Faith Based and Community Initiatives
Indiana Government Center South, Room E012
302 West Washington Street
Indianapolis, IN 46204
www.in.gov/ofbci

Iowa

Iowa Commission on Volunteer Service
200 East Grand Avenue
Des Moines, IA 50309
www.volunteeriowa.org

Kansas

Kansas Office for Community Service
120 Southeast Tenth Ave
Topeka, KS 66612
www.kanserve.org

Kentucky

Kentucky Commission on Community Volunteerism and
  Service
275 East Main Street, Mail Stop 3W-F
Frankfort, KY 40621
www.chfs.ky.gov/dhss/kccvs

Louisiana

Louisiana Service Commission
263 Third Street, Suite 610B
Baton Rouge, LA 70801
www.crt.state.la.us/laserve

Maine

Maine Commission for Community Service
Maine State Planning Office
187 State Street
38 State House Station
Augusta, ME 04333
www.maineservicecommission.gov

Manitoba

Volunteer Centre of Winnipeg
410-5 Donald Street South
Winnipeg, MB R3L 2T4
Canada
www.volunteerwinnipeg.mb.ca

Maryland

Governor's Office on Service and Volunteerism
State Office Center
301 West Preston Street, Suite 1502L
Baltimore, MD 21201
www.gosv.state.md.us

Massachusetts
Massachusetts Service Alliance
100 North Washington Street, Third Floor
Boston, MA 02114
www.mass-service.org

Michigan
Michigan Community Service Commission
1048 Pierpont, Suite 4
Lansing, MI 48913
www.michigan.gov/mcsc

Mississippi
Mississippi Commission for Volunteer Services
3825 Ridgewood Road, Suite 601
Jackson, MS 39211
www.mcvs.org

Missouri
Missouri Community Service Commission
770 Truman State Office Building
PO Box 118
Jefferson City, MO 65102
www.movolunteers.org

Nebraska
Nebraska Volunteer Service Commission
State Capitol, Sixth Floor West
PO Box 98927
Lincoln, NE 68509
www.nvsc.ne.gov

Nevada

Nevada Commission for National and Community Service
137 Keedie Street
Fallon, NV 89406
www.ncncs.org

New Hampshire

Office of Volunteerism
117 Pleasant Street
Dolloff Building
Concord, NH 03301
www.volunteernh.org

New Jersey

Governor's Office of Volunteerism
225 West State Street
PO Box 456
Trenton, NJ 08625
www.state.nj.us/state/njvolunteerism

New Mexico

New Mexico Commission for Community Volunteerism
3401 Pan American Freeway NE
Albuquerque, NM 87107
www.newmexserve.org

New York

New York State Commission on National and Community
  Services
52 Washington Street
Rensselaer, NY 12144
www.ocfs.state.ny.us/main/Youth/nyscncs

North Carolina

North Carolina Commission on Volunteerism and
  Community Service
Office of the Governor
20312 Mail Service Center
116 West Jones Street
Raleigh, NC 27699
www.volunteernc.org

North Dakota

Share Network
Job Service North Dakota
PO Box 55007
Bismarck, ND 58506
www.sharenetworknd.com

Ohio

Ohio Community Service Council
51 North High Street, Suite 800
Columbus, OH 43215
www.serveohio.org

Oklahoma

Community Services Commission
1401 North Lincoln Boulevard
Oklahoma City, OK 73104
www.okamericorps.com

Ontario

Volunteer Opportunity Exchange
330 Gilmour Street
Ottawa, ON K2P 2P6
Canada
www.voe-reb.org

Oregon
Oregon Student Assistance Commission
1500 Valley River Drive, Suite100
Eugene, OR 97401
www.aspireoregon.org

Pennsylvania
PennSERVE: Governor's Office of Citizen's Service
PennSERVE
1306 Labor & Industry Building
Seventh and Forster Streets
Harrisburg, PA 17120
www.dli.state.pa.us/pennserve

Rhode Island
Volunteer Center of Rhode Island
55 Bradford Street, Suite 302
Providence, RI 02903
www.vcri.org

South Carolina
Governor's Office of Executive Policy and Programs
1205 Pendleton Street
Columbia, SC 29201
www.govoepp.state.sc.us

South Dakota
Volunteers of America, South Dakota
PO Box 89306
Sioux Falls, SD 57109
www.voa.org

Tennessee

Tennessee Commission on National and Community Services
Department of Finance & Administration
Tennessee State Capitol
Nashville, TN 37243
www.state.tn.us/finance/rds/tcncs.htm

Texas

OneStar Foundation
816 Congress, Suite 900
Austin, TX 78701
www.onestarfoundation.org

Utah

Utah Commission on Volunteers
324 South State Street, Suite 500
Salt Lake City, UT 84111
www.volunteers.utah.gov

Vermont

Vermont Commission on National and Community Service
109 State Street
Montpelier, VT 05609
www.state.vt.us/cncs

Virginia

Virginia Office on Volunteerism and Community Service
7 North Eighth Street, Fifth Floor
Richmond, VA 23219
www.dss.state.va.us/community

Washington

Washington State Commission for National and Community
Service
PO Box 43113
Olympia, WA 98504
www.ofm.wa.gov/servewa

West Virginia

West Virginia Commission for National and Community
Service
601 Delaware Avenue
Charleston, WV 25302
www.connectwv.org

Wisconsin

Wisconsin Department of Health and Family Services
One West Wilson Street
Madison, WI 53703
www.dhfs.wisconsin.gov

Wyoming

Volunteers of America of Wyoming
PO Box 6291
2 North Main, Suite 201
Sheridan, WY 82801
www.voa.org

Employers of International Consultants

United States

Advanced Technology Ventures
485 Ramona Street, Suite 200
Palo Alto, CA 94301
www.atvcapital.com

Adventist Development and Relief Agency International
12501 Old Columbia Pike
Silver Spring, MD 20904
www.adra.org

The Asia Foundation
465 California Street, Ninth Floor
San Francisco, CA 94104
www.asiafoundation.org

Associates in Rural Development, Inc.
159 Bank Street, Suite 300
Burlington, VT 05401
www.ardinc.com/careers

Berger, Louis, International, Inc.
100 Halsted Street
East Orange, NJ 07018
www.louisberger.com

Black and Veatch, Engineers-Architects
8400 Ward Parkway
Overland Park, KS 66204
www.bv.com

Catholic Relief Services
PO Box 17090
Baltimore, MD 21203
www.crs.org

CARE-Cooperative
151 Ellis Street NE
Atlanta, GA 30303
www.care.org

Cooperative Housing Foundation International
8601 Georgia Avenue, Suite 800
Silver Spring, MD 20910
www.chfhq.org

Education Developmental Center
55 Chapel Street
Newton, MA 02458
www.edc.org

Family Health International
PO Box 13950
Research Triangle Park, NC 27709
www.fhi.org

International Executive Service Corps
1900 M Street, Suite 500
Washington, DC 20036
www.iesc.org

International Food Policy Research Institute
2033 K Street NW
Washington, DC 20006
www.ifpri.org

Helen Keller International, Inc.
352 Park Avenue South, Twelfth Floor
New York, NY 10010
www.hki.org

Arthur D Little., Inc.
125 High Street, Twenty-Eighth Floor
Boston, MA 02110
www.adlittle-us.com

Nathan Associates, Inc.
2101 Wilson Boulevard, Suite 1200
Arlington, VA 22201
www.nathanassoc.com

National Academy of Science
500 Fifth Street NW
Washington, DC 20001
www.nasonline.org

Parsons Brinckerhoff
One Penn Plaza
New York, NY 10119
www.pbworld.com

Pathfinder International
Nine Galen Street, Suite 217
Watertown, MA 02472
www.pathfind.org

Project Hope
255 Carter Hall Lane
Millwood, VA 22646
www.projhope.org

Planning and Development Collaborative International
  (PADCO)
1025 Thomas Jefferson Street NW, Suite 170
Washington, DC 20007
www. padco.aecom.com

Population Council
One Dag Hammarskjold Plaza
New York, NY 10017
www.popcouncil.org

Population Reference Bureau
1875 Connecticut Avenue NW, Suite 520
Washington, DC 20009
www.prb.org

Pragma Systems Corporation
1810 Samuel Morse Drive
Reston, VA 20190
www.pragmasystems.com

Price Waterhouse Coopers LLP
300 Madison Avenue
New York, NY 10017
www.pw.com

Research Triangle Institute
PO Box 12194
Research Triangle Park, NC 27709
www.rti.org

Save the Children Federation
54 Wilton Road
Westport, CT 06880
www.savethechildren.org

Spanish Education Development Center
1840 Kalorama Road NW
Washington, DC 20009
www.sedcenter.org

United Nations Childrens Fund (UNICEF)
Three United Nations Plaza
New York, NY 10017
www.unicef.org

U.S. Fund for UNICEF
333 East Thirty-Eighth Street
Mail Code GC-6
New York, NY 10016
www.unicef.org

Urban Institute
2100 M Street NW
Washington, DC 20037
www.urban.org

World Wildlife Fund
1250 Twenty-Fourth Street NW
PO Box 97180
Washington, DC 20090
www.worldwildlife.org

Trade Offices
U.S. Chamber of Commerce
1615 H Street NW
Washington, DC 20062
www.uschamber.com

Consulate Trade Offices are located in Cleveland, Ohio; Buffalo,
New York; Princeton, New Jersey; and San Francisco and San Jose,
California.

Canada

Cultural-Political Organizations
Association for Canadian Studies in the United States
1220 Nineteenth Street NW, Suite 801
Washington, DC 20036
www.acsus.org

U.S. Embassy in Ottawa
207 Bank Street, Suite 418
Ottawa, ON K2P 2N2
Canada
http://canada.usembassy.gov

Foreign Affairs and International Trade Canada
125 Sussex Drive
Ottawa, ON K1A 0G2
Canada
www.international.gc.ca

Canadian Consulates in the United States

Embassy of Canada
501 Pennsylvania Avenue NW
Washington, DC 20001
www.canadianembassy.org

Consulate General of Canada
550 South Hope Street, Ninth Floor
Los Angeles, CA 90071
www.geo.international.gc.ca

Consulate General of Canada
580 California Street, Fourteenth Floor
San Francisco, CA 94104
www.geo.international.gc.ca

Consulate General of Canada
First Union Financial Center, Suite 1600
200 South Biscayne Boulevard
Miami, FL 33131
www.geo.international.gc.ca

Consulate General of Canada
1175 Peachtree Street
100 Colony Square, Suite 1700
Atlanta, GA 30361
www.geo.international.gc.ca

Consulate General of Canada
Two Prudential Plaza
180 North Stetson Avenue, Suite 2400
Chicago, IL 60601
www.geo.international.gc.ca

Consulate General of Canada
Three Copley Place, Suite 400
Boston, MA 02116
www.geo.international.gc.ca

Consulate General of Canada
1625 Broadway, Suite 2600
Denver, CO 80202
www.geo.international.gc.ca

Consulate General of Canada
600 Renaissance Center, Suite 1100
Detroit, MI 48243
www.geo.international.gc.ca

Consulate General of Canada
701 Fourth Avenue South, Suite 901
Minneapolis, MN 55415
www.geo.international.gc.ca

Consulate General of Canada
1251 Avenue of the Americas
New York, NY 10020
www.geo.international.gc.ca

Consulate General of Canada
750 North St. Paul Street, Suite 1700
Dallas, TX 75201
www.geo.international.gc.ca

Consulate General of Canada
1504 Fourth Avenue, Suite 600
Seattle, WA 98101
www.geo.international.gc.ca

About the Authors

J. Laurence Day is Professor Emeritus, University of West Florida, where he taught journalism for twelve years. In 2000, Day retired and became a lecturer at the University of Kansas, where he had been a professor at the William Allen White School of Journalism for twenty-two years. He earned B.A. and M.A. degrees at Brigham Young University and a Ph.D. at the University of Minnesota. Day has been a foreign correspondent in Latin America and a reporter and copyeditor for U.S. metropolitan newspapers. His career research interests included professionalization of Latin American journalists and international news flow, about which he has published extensively. He has held three senior Fulbright overseas lectureships, taught at fifteen universities in Latin America, and conducted workshops for journalists in Africa and throughout Latin America and the Caribbean. He was on a team that produced the television documentaries "Giving Up the Canal," "Campaign for Cuba," and "Cuba: The End of the Revolution." With H. Ned Seelye, he produced nine anti–drug abuse comic books that were published in English and Spanish and distributed nationwide to at-risk young people.

Margaret C. Day holds an M.A. in Library Science from Emporia State University and a B.A. in education from Brigham Young University. She was an elementary school librarian/media specialist for twenty years in Lawrence, Kansas, and Pensacola, Florida. Her travels include Europe, Asia, and the Far East. She traveled widely in Latin America and twice lived in Argentina. She served as researcher, copyeditor, and proofreader in the preparation of this third edition.

H. Ned Seelye was lead author on the first edition of *Careers for Foreign Language Aficionados and Other Multilingual Types*, published in 1991. Ned quit high school at the end of his junior year and hitchhiked to Mexico to seek his fortune. From that inauspicious beginning he went on to become a national and international expert in intercultural communication and educational research. His international career included projects in thirty countries. He was an author, university anthropology professor, and business executive. H. Ned Seelye died in November 1997.